HUMMINGBIRDS

BY

CRAWFORD H. GREENEWALT

FOREWORD BY

DEAN AMADON

DOVER PUBLICATIONS, INC., NEW YORK

Drawings of birds by Dale Astle were in all instances made from photographs taken by the author. Except for obvious decorative vignettes and where otherwise indicated, they are shown at life size.

Published in Canada by General Publishing Company, Ltd., 30 Lesmill Road, Don Mills, Toronto, Ontario.

Published in the United Kingdom by Constable and Company, Ltd., 3 The Lanchesters, 162–164 Fulham Palace Road, London W6 9ER.

This Dover edition, first published in 1990, is an unabridged, slightly rearranged republication of the work first published for the American Museum of Natural History by Doubleday & Company, Garden City, New York, 1960. For this edition the decorative tan background of some of the illustrations has been eliminated or reproduced in gray, and the location of some illustrations has been changed, including those constituting the portfolio of color photographs, which has been rearranged to fit into 52 pages (rather than 138 pages as before; no text or photograph has been eliminated, however, and the photographs remain life-size). The frontispiece has been moved to page 101, and the set of color photographs now appearing in black and white on page 30 (formerly page 172, where it previously appeared in color) has been reproduced in color on page 102. Many page numbers have been changed and the index revised.

Manufactured in the United States of America
Dover Publications, Inc., 31 East 2nd Street, Mineola, N.Y. 11501

Library of Congress Cataloging-in-Publication Data

Greenewalt, Crawford H., 1902–
   Hummingbirds / by Crawford H. Greenewalt ; foreword by Dean Amadon.
      p.   cm.
   Reprint. Originally published: Garden City, N.Y. : Published for the American Museum of Natural History by Doubleday, 1960.
   Includes index.
   ISBN 0-486-26431-9
   1. Hummingbirds—Western Hemisphere.   2. Hummingbirds—Western Hemisphere—Pictorial works.   I. Title.
QL696.A558G73   1990
598′.899—dc20
                                                                                    90-42723
                                                                                    CIP

FOREWORD

To the American bird watcher, whose ranks have reached extraordinary proportions in recent years, the name "hummingbird" usually recalls a bird known from personal experience. The fact is, however, that the sample afforded North Americans represents but a small fraction of the hundreds of species and gives but a modest hint of the brilliant plumage and the broad range of color and form which characterize this remarkable group. Out of some three hundred species, only a dozen or so are native to the United States, and east of the Mississippi there is only one.

Most of the known varieties are indigenous to the Equatorial regions of South America, spreading both north and south from their ancestral headquarters in Amazonia or the Andes. The North American varieties are not without charm, and some are very colorful, while many of South America's are as drab as a sparrow. Nonetheless, it is in the tropics that the color spectrum becomes really spectacular and the elaboration of ornamental plumes luxuriates. Unfortunately, with the remoteness of these areas, many species, including some of the most exotic, are virtually unknown as living birds.

The literature of hummingbirds, so far as mere description is concerned, is reasonably full. The most conspicuous deficiency is in visual presentation. The best known is John Gould's great study, five imperial folio volumes with three hundred hand-colored plates. It is now more than a century old and may be seen only by appointment in a few libraries and museums. The Gould plates are remarkably authentic considering the handicap of the artist, an Englishman, who was obliged to work from skins rather than from live models. Other painters have made attractive renderings also, but most have been influenced more by decorative than scientific considerations.

Against such a background, Crawford H. Greenewalt's monograph with its superb portfolio of color photographs becomes an event of much importance, destined, we may confidently predict, to become a classic of natural history. While photographs of North American hummingbirds have been published in modest numbers, no study covering any substantial segment of the family has ever been attempted. Most of the species here shown are exposed to the camera for the first time; their remote habitat alone has precluded serious attention by earlier photographers. No individual has ever before seen, much less photographed, so wide a range of the species. Mr. Greenewalt's ultra high-speed photographs are the result of a highly developed technical skill, plus an artist's feeling for color and form. They represent at once a technical achievement and an artistic triumph.

HUMMINGBIRDS is, however, far more than a vicarious birdwalk, for it is the scientific contribution that insures for this book a really definitive status. Mr. Greenewalt has brought to his study the enthusiasm and the organizing capacity which have made him one of America's top industrial executives. Characteristically, he has combined sound and imaginative scholarship with advanced technological methods to reach new and exciting conclusions.

The exact nature of the optical phenomena responsible for the hummingbird's iridescent colors, for example, has been little understood. Studying the complex feather structure with the techniques of the modern research laboratory, Mr. Greenewalt demonstrates the underlying principles for the first time. To his study of flight aerodynamics he brought specially designed, high-speed equipment which verifies data formerly subject largely to speculation.

For millions of years, hummingbirds have been rocketing from blossom to blossom through the jungles, usually beyond the ken of either naturalist or casual traveler. Only now, thanks to Mr. Greenewalt, are we able to enjoy their beauty in full and to comprehend the incredibly precise adaptations—the result of long ages of natural selection—embodied in the members of this unique ornithological family.

Dean Amadon
Lamont Curator of Birds
The American Museum of Natural History

PREFACE

I photographed my first hummingbird one sultry summer afternoon in 1953. It was a male ruby throat, come for courtship to Delaware after a bachelor's winter in Mexico. I had read of the hummingbird's extremely rapid wing beat and was interested primarily in seeing whether a technique I had developed for photographing small birds in flight would produce satisfactory results with these darting acrobats. To my surprise, wing action was adequately "stopped" and the pictures were charming and much admired. So it was that I caught hummingbird fever.

I knew rather vaguely that there were many species, most of them in South America. As my interest grew, I pored over the delightful but somewhat idealized engravings in the two volumes of Jardine's NATURAL HISTORY (published in 1833) which deal with hummingbirds. Photographs existed for only a few North American species. It seems to me now an act of complete and utter rashness to have gone then, as I did, to the American Museum of Natural History to ask whether there would be interest in a series of photographs representative of the various species, to be published with an appropriate text. At the outset, I could offer only a handful of pictures of a single species and an abysmal ornithological ignorance, adequately neutralized (I thought and hoped) by unbounded enthusiasm. The Museum staff was kind enough to express keen interest and my fever reached an advanced stage.

Now it is 1960 and the task is complete. Perhaps if I had known what the intervening years were to bring, I would not have had the courage to begin. The photographs presented here involved traveling some one hundred thousand miles in visiting perhaps a half dozen countries and regions. There were three trips each to Brazil and Ecuador, two to Venezuela, and excursions to Cuba, Jamaica, Panama, Arizona, California and Colorado. Each voyage had its quota of adventure, triumph and frustration.

Whatever I might have done in prospect, in retrospect I wouldn't have missed a mile, nor an hour, anywhere along the way.

A preface customarily gives acknowledgment of assistance or inspiration in bringing the author's effort to a reasonable conclusion. This convention poses for me a difficult problem. I am not an expert in ornithology, electronics, photography, or even in the geography of hummingbird habitats. I have, therefore, enlisted the help of countless individuals who have given advice and assistance unstintingly and to whom I owe a great debt. My dilemma arises out of the fact that, if I listed them all here and indicated the nature of their contribution, this preface would become a text in itself, and a long one at that.

I have resolved the matter by presenting my collaborators in an appendix, and I hope they will understand that their being relegated to the back of the book diminishes neither my sense of obligation nor my gratitude.

To this I must make two exceptions, the first being a very special appreciation to Dr. Augusto Ruschi, Director of the Museu Mello-Leitão at Santa Teresa, Espírito Santo, in Brazil. Without Dr. Ruschi's cheerful and unfailing assistance, the portfolio of photographs presented herein would have been much smaller and less inclusive.

In his aviary at Santa Teresa, more than a hundred birds, representing forty or more species, lead completely normal lives. Many species feed, bathe, court and breed just as they do in the wild. Hundreds more come to his outdoor feeders. He has been kind enough to collect living birds for me in Brazil, Ecuador and Venezuela, and the fact that I have been able to photograph more than a hundred species is largely due to his efforts.

Dr. Ruschi is, I am sure, the world's leading expert on living hummingbirds. A visit with him is a memorable and rewarding experience. I look forward to many more and to the enjoyment his hospitality, keen interest, and intimate knowledge will bring.

I must also record my great obligation to Mr. Victor F. Hanson who, together with his associates, is largely responsible for the equipment with which these photographs were taken. However unreasonable my demands for some new electronic gadget, they were filled completely and more often than not with embellishments well beyond the best performance to which I had aspired.

I recall complaining bitterly about the wear and tear on arms and back in carrying an automobile storage battery over hill and dale to supply the necessary electrical energy in the field. Mr. Hanson merely asked whether "next week" would be soon enough for a light-weight alternate. This incidentally involved a complete redesign of a substantial part of the electronic flash units.

Who could possibly fail to carry through a project, however difficult, with such competent and willing assistance?

One final word. Color and mode of flight are beautifully characteristic for hummingbirds. As my interest grew, I could not resist delving into the scientific basis for both phenomena. The results will be presented elsewhere in correct technical language and with the scientific i's and t's dotted and crossed. Here I have endeavored to tell the story simply and concisely, hoping that it will be of sufficient general interest to justify the reader's attention.

Crawford H. Greenewalt
Greenville, Delaware

CONTENTS

FOREWORD
    By Dean Amadon iii

PREFACE v

CHAPTER 1
    Behavior and Characteristics 1

CHAPTER 2
    Feathers, Color and Iridescence 27

A PHOTOGRAPHIC PORTFOLIO
    Index of Plates 50

CHAPTER 3
    Flight 113

CHAPTER 4
    Methods and Equipment 149

ACKNOWLEDGMENTS 160

INDEX 162

Distribution of Hummingbird Species by Latitudinal Zones...

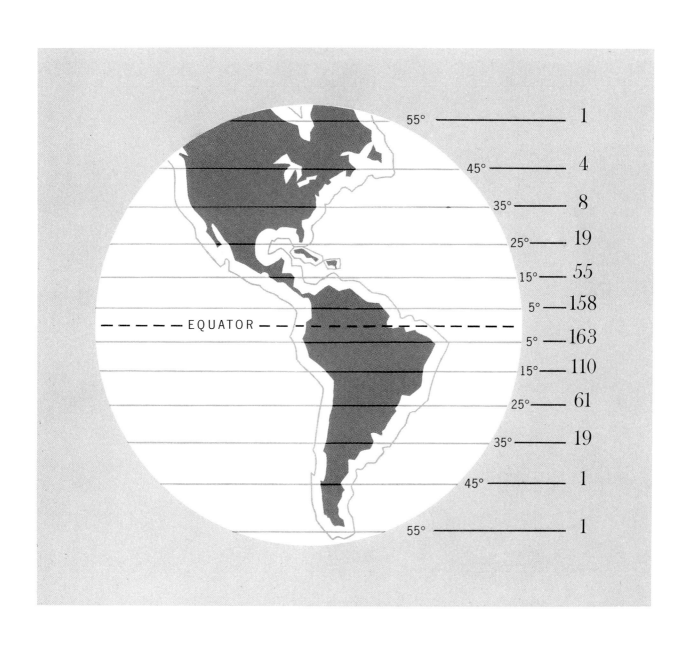

chapter 1

BEHAVIOR AND CHARACTERISTICS

What is a hummingbird?

A sound definition always seems like a good, or at least an obvious, start in any quest for enlightenment. When I first became interested in hummingbirds a few years ago, I put the question to my ornithological friends, hoping that the answer would pave the way to greater knowledge and understanding.

Here is what they supplied, as embodied in Professor Charles Sibley's highly reputable compilation:

SUBORDER TROCHILI—HUMMINGBIRDS

Schizognathous anisodactyle Apodiformes with 8 pairs of ribs; bill long and slender, gape not deeply cleft; tibial bridge absent; nostrils lateral, broadly operculate; tongue extensile; secondaries 6-7; alular feathers 0-1; aftershaft small or absent; 14-15 cervical vertebrae; syrinx with 2 pairs of special intrinsic muscles; no sterno-tracheal muscles; nestling with spherical crop; caeca rudimentary or absent; no gall bladder; no adult down; diastataxic in most, some eutaxic; no claw on manus.

Even though "gape not deeply cleft" has a fine Shakespearean swing, I must say that the definition leaves the lay student little wiser. I was obliged to seek further.

Without their working clothes, ornithologists become much more lyrical. Alexander Wilson, the earliest American ornithologist—and no mean poet—had this to say:

"What heavenly tints in mingling radiance fly!
    Each rapid movement gives a different dye;
Like scales of burnished gold they dazzling show—
    Now sink to shade, now like a furnace glow!"

To Audubon, the hummingbird was a "glittering fragment of the rainbow . . . a lovely little creature moving on humming winglets through the air, suspended as if by magic in it, flitting from one flower to another, with motions as graceful as they are light and airy, pursuing its course and yielding new delights whenever it is seen."

Sir William Jardine introduces his monograph on hummingbirds, published in 1833, with the following lines:

"His silken vest was purfled o'er with green,
    And crimson rose-leaves wrought the sprigs between;
His diadem, a topaz, beam'd so bright,
    The moon was dazzled with its purest light."

Buffon, a French naturalist of the eighteenth century, considered hummingbirds "of all animated beings . . . the most elegant in form and brilliant in color. The stones and metals polished by art are not comparable to this gem of nature. She has placed it in the order of birds, but among the tiniest of the race . . . she has loaded it with all the gifts of which she has only given other birds a share."

Much more pleasant and far less alarming than *schizognathous anisodactyle Apodiformes!*

The common name of the family varies with the country of origin.

We call them hummingbirds, which certainly does not do justice to

Audubon's lyric description. The French, with uncharacteristic lack of imagination, say *oiseau-mouche,* or fly-sized bird. The Spanish and Portuguese do a bit better with *pica flor* (peck the flower) and *beija flor* (kiss the flower). In the Antilles they are called *murmures,* the murmurers; and in Cuba, *zum-zum* (phonetically an apt description).

The Indian populations of Central and South American countries have done a great deal better. Their common names, *ourissa, huitzitzil, guanumbia, quinde,* signify "rays of the sun," "tresses of the day-star," and the like. Even in scientific nomenclature, the sun, the stars, and precious stones appear frequently. The genus *Heliomaster,* for example, or "lord of the sun"; *Topaza pyra,* the "fiery topaz"; *Stellula,* the "little star"; *Chrysolampis,* the "golden torch"; *Sapphirina,* the "sapphire."

All of this begs the original question: "What is a hummingbird?" As a layman's try, with all proper apologies to Professor Sibley, I would say that if you see a very small bird hovering, body motionless, before a flower—then you have seen a hummingbird, whether you are in Saskatchewan, Ecuador, or Tierra del Fuego. It is the method of flight that is unique. All hummingbirds hover; no other bird hovers as consistently or as efficiently.

Hummingbirds are creatures of the Western Hemisphere. They are found in North, Central, and South America, and in the Islands of the Caribbean—nowhere else. Why this should be so is another of Nature's mysteries. Since they are small and of limited endurance it is not surprising that they have found the ocean barriers too difficult. They do, however, adapt themselves to many climates and there is every reason to believe that they would be able to enjoy life in the mountains, forests, and deserts of, let us say, Africa as well as they have done in South America. The element of chance in the evolutionary process is, however, of such overwhelming importance that repetition of the sequence leading to the hummingbird in some other part of the world must be counted a biological impossibility.

There are many species and subspecies. Just how many is difficult to state precisely. This is because the classifiers over the years have changed designations as new relationships became apparent with the result that subspecies and species have been added, eliminated or shifted. The last comprehensive survey of the family was made by James Lee Peters in his "Check List of the Birds of the World" (1945). He recognizes 121 genera, 319 species and 656 forms. I wouldn't, however, count on this as the final answer.

The geographical distribution of species varies with the latitude, the largest number being found within a band 5 degrees north and south of the Equator. In Canada, four species are known to breed. This number increases as one goes south and reaches its peak of 163 in the vicinity of the Equator, then diminishes again to four or five species in southern Argentina and Chile. The geocenter of the family, if that is a proper term to use in this connection, is in the country of Ecuador where almost half of the known species are found.

In the vertical plane their distribution is also wide. There is a genus in South America found only at altitudes between 12,000 and 15,000 feet; in fact there is one form, *Oreotrochilus chimborazo chimborazo*,* found only on Mount Chimborazo in Ecuador. This one never descends from its heights to mingle with its kinsmen at lower levels, remaining within a few thousand feet of the equatorial snowline.

There are hummingbirds at all altitudes and in all climates—there are birds of the forest, of the garden, of the plains, of the mountains, and of the desert; in fact one can say that wherever and whenever flowers bloom in the western world hummingbirds will be found. A ubiquitous and adaptable family.

Perhaps I should say a special word about the species of the United States. In the entire area east of the Mississippi there is only one species—the ruby throat (*Archilochus colubris*)—which most easterners see in their gardens during spring and summer. The west does quite

4

*Readers will have to get used to this, I'm afraid. Hummingbird species rarely have common names, and can only be properly identified by their scientific appellations, formidable as they are.

CANADA

SELASPHORUS RUFUS

ARCHILOCHUS COLUBRIS

PACIFIC OCEAN

UNITED STATES

ATLANTIC OCEAN

SOUTH AMERICA

BREEDING AND WINTERING RANGES

Selasphorus rufus
and
Archilochus colubris

a bit better, with eleven breeding species, but several of these barely get across the Mexican border. While this is a pretty poor showing—twelve out of three hundred odd—as beauty goes we do quite well. All of our hummingbirds are colorful and gay and none of them has the rather somber appearance of some of their South American relatives.

As a general rule hummingbirds do not migrate, but as with most rules there are notable exceptions. The vast majority of species spend their lives within a relatively limited area. As long as flowers bloom they are content, feeling no urge to wander. The notable exceptions are three birds that breed in North America—the ruby throat in the east and the rufous and calliope in the west. Ruby throat and rufous migrate at least two thousand miles from breeding site to winter quarters. How they can manage it still remains something of a mystery. Without doubt they do indeed manage, and apparently without great numerical losses. The ruby throat is even said to cross the Gulf of Mexico, a distance of five hundred miles—a remarkable accomplishment indeed for a creature whose length measures scarcely three inches.

The migration of hummingbirds that live south of the Equator has not been exhaustively studied. There is, however, one Chilean spe-

Ocreatus underwoodii ♂

TAILS

Trochilus polytmus ♂

cies, *Sephanoides sephanoides,* which has a range extending from 23 degrees south latitude south to the Straits of Magellan and beyond at about 54 degrees south latitude. (Curiously enough, this equals almost exactly the latitudinal range of the ruby throat in the north.) It seems fairly clear that in Southern Hemisphere winters, *Sephanoides* migrates northward from the colder part of its range in the south, going even beyond the area where it regularly nests.

The hummingbird family is notable for its contradictions. The student seeking neatly packaged classifications encounters so many confusing exceptions that categorical observations are continually subject to challenge. While pondering definitions, I considered the possibility of using as a criterion the brilliant iridescent colors, considered to be a sort of trademark for the family. Unfortunately not all hummingbirds are brilliantly colored. Most of the females, for example, are relatively dull, although a few are quite as gorgeous as their consorts. To make matters more difficult, there are several genera and a good many species in which both female and male have subdued, sparrow-like colors. While it is quite proper to say that if you see a very small bird with highly iridescent colors you have seen a hummingbird, there are so many that have no

Archilochus colubris ♀

Popelairia langsdorffi ♂

Tail feathers vary widely, from the tiny fans at the far left to the spectacular long "streamer," left center. The type at far right is the dainty "thorn tail" while the female ruby throat at right center depicts the more conventional equipment.

iridescence that the definition omits more birds than it includes.

When the iridescent colors do occur they are really striking, and Audubon's characterization "glittering fragment of the rainbow" is, if anything, an understatement. No other bird is so brilliant.

There are two notable things about these colors. The first is that they are structural and not pigmentary.* The second is that they are highly directional and in a living bird one must have a quick eye to see them at all. In the next chapter there will be a more detailed discussion of iridescent colors, their directional character, and the particular structure which produces them.

Let me say only that for the iridescence to be seen the bird must be facing the light, which must also be behind the observer. Under these conditions the colors flash out in brilliant rays astonishing in their intensity and beauty. Let the bird turn its head just a few degrees and the colors disappear. This is why a quick eye is needed, but patient observation will be amply rewarded.

To residents of the United States the colors will be largely reds and purples. Farther south the spectrum enlarges and the colors cover the whole range from brilliant red to brilliant blue, with all of the intervening possibilities of hue and shade.

I had once thought also of using size as a criterion for defining hummingbirds. It is quite true that the family includes the smallest bird known to man. This is *Calypte helenae,* a Cuban hummingbird called the "bee," a tiny creature about 2¼ inches long. Many other hummingbirds, perhaps two-thirds of the species, are smaller than the smallest birds of other families, but here again there are exceptions—so many in fact that size alone will not make a useful definition. The largest hummingbird is *Patagona gigas,* an inhabitant of the Andes, about 8½ inches in length and roughly equal in bulk to a good-sized swift. Hummingbirds, then, can certainly be called "small," but by no means are they invariably the "smallest" of the avian population.

*The blue sky, a rainbow, a drop of oil on a wet pavement, the brilliant flash from a diamond are structural colors; a red tie, a blue dress are pigmentary.

Perhaps the most extraordinary thing about the hummingbird is its power plant. For living animals zoologists use the word metabolism to define energy output. The measurement of human metabolism is usually a diagnostic tool for physicians, but basically metabolism for living things is equivalent to the horsepower of an automobile engine or the kilowatt rating for an electric range.

Hummingbirds have the highest energy output per unit of weight of any living warm-blooded animal. In discussing their extraordinary activity, figures are fairly meaningless unless they can be related to something we all recognize. For that reason I will use humans as a standard of reference — not a valid scientific comparison, perhaps, but one which will be understandable.

A hummingbird while hovering has an energy output per unit weight about ten times that of a man running nine miles an hour. This is pretty close to the highest possible output of human energy and a pace that can be maintained no longer than half an hour. A hummingbird, on the other hand, can fly for much longer periods. A man doing the same work per unit weight would be expending 40 horsepower!

A man's actual daily energy output is about 3,500 calories. The daily output of a hummingbird leading its ordinary life — eating, flying, perching, sleeping—if calculated for a 170-pound man is equivalent to about 155,000 calories.

If we convert these figures to food intake the results are astonishing. A normal man will consume two to two and a half pounds of food per day. If his energy output were that of a hummingbird, he would have to consume during the day 285 pounds of hamburger, or 370 pounds of boiled potatoes, or 130 pounds of bread!

Actually hummingbirds use sugar as their principal food and sugar has a much higher energy content than any of the items listed here for the human larder. Even so the average hummingbird consumes half its weight of sugar daily, an extraordinary intake.

Let me recite one more statistic. The hummingbird's surface temperature is normally slightly higher than ours. If a man were expending energy at the rate of a hovering hummingbird, and could perspire freely, he would have to evaporate about one hundred pounds of perspiration per hour to keep his skin temperature below the boiling point of water. If his water supply ran out, his skin temperature would rise to 750°F., well above the melting point of lead, at which temperature he would glow, and probably ignite. There is much to be said for our relatively sedentary existence.

Hummingbirds must feed abundantly and regularly to keep up their energy supply. If artificial feeders are provided, they come in for their snack once every ten or fifteen minutes. We humans can get along on a charge of fuel three times a day—hummingbirds, relatively speaking, must refuel almost continuously.

After all this, it might well be asked what they do at night. Here Nature, with her customary ingenuity, has found an unusually elegant solution. She has given the birds the ability to pass into a state of suspended animation, during which the body temperature drops and the energy output sinks to a very low figure. In this state the birds can be handled without their taking the slightest notice. The factors inducing them to enter this torpid condition are not yet completely understood. Confusingly, it is not a nightly occurrence, nor is it necessarily associated with low temperatures.

My own view is that passage into torpor is in some way connected with the energy reserves of the bird at nightfall. If, for example, the bird has fed well during the day and its energy reserves are high, it will sleep normally. If, however, food is scarce and our bird goes to its slumber without sufficient nourishment, it will stretch out its available energy reserves by becoming torpid. Arousal from the torpid state is extremely rapid and almost before you know it the birds are wide awake and eager for their morning meal.

AWAKE AND ASLEEP

The two drawings here represent the day and night posture of the same bird, the elegant Boissonneaua jardini. *At bedtime the hummingbird merely contracts his neck, scrunches his shoulders down, ruffles his feathers and is off to sleep. He awakens instantly alert.*

Boissonneaua jardini ♂

The energy output of the bird when torpid is only one-twentieth that associated with normal sleep. If this seems to get them back into the human area, let me say that even in the torpid state they still put out about as much energy proportionately as a man taking his early morning constitutional.

The ability of hummingbirds to pass into coma seems to have been known for many years. Father Bernabe Cobo, a Spanish priest, wrote in 1653 in his "Historia del Nuevo Mundo" that the "awakening" of hummingbirds was used as evidence by the Mexican Jesuits in explaining the mystery of the Resurrection to the Indians. In a more temporal mood, the good Father goes on to say,

"I have heard that Chilean ladies hasten the resurrection of hummingbirds by sheltering them in their bosoms. Hence — and with no need for mystic metaphors — they have come to call them 'Resurrected' birds."

In view of the high energy requirement, getting the necessary fifty or sixty meals a day is a pretty pressing problem. For this also they are well equipped. They have a very unusual and highly extensible tongue with which they can reach deep into a flower for their supply of nectar. The tongue is tubular, and with what must be very much like an internal suction pump they can consume their fuel quickly, efficiently, and in adequate abundance.

So far we have discussed only the energy requirement of hummingbirds but of course they, like us, must have a diet containing an adequate balance of proteins, fats, and vitamins. As to these dietary supplements, there are no substantial differences between their needs and those of other warm-blooded animals. A dog, a chicken, or a man must consume about 1/1000th of the weight of the body in protein per day, and, while the evidence is by no means conclusive, hummingbirds appear to need no more.

Here, however, is the evidence: Dr. Augusto Ruschi, as expert about hummingbirds as anyone alive, placed a small bird (*Calliphlox amethystina* to be exact) in a muslin-covered cage with an abundant supply of sugar solution. During the course of a day he introduced fruit flies one by one until the bird, presumably sated, would take no more. He records that ten to fifteen fruit flies were consumed. A fruit fly weighs about one one-thousandth of a gram, the bird two and eight-tenths grams, and so, making due allowance for that part of the fruit fly useless as a dietary supplement, hummingbirds and humans are not far apart in their protein intake.

Whatever the validity of this experiment, it seems clear that hummingbirds obtain their dietary supplements entirely from insects and spiders, and an occasional capture would appear to afford a properly balanced diet. In taking flying insects the extraordinary tongue of the hummingbird seems not to be used. They pursue and capture their victims using the beak in much the same way as any other bird.

The hummingbird power plant leads us quite naturally to what we might call their "migratory fuel supply." Few hummingbirds migrate but those that do show an astonishing capacity to put on fat against the period of their strenuous migratory exertions. Studies made of the ruby throat immediately before migration indicate that this little bird can add fifty per cent to its normal weight, all of it fat, to provide an extra fuel tank, so to speak, for its long, nonstop flight across the Gulf of Mexico. To make once again a human comparison, it is as if a 170-pound man could in a few weeks put on enough fat to increase his weight to 255 pounds, against some extraordinary and short period of exertion during which he could neither eat nor sleep.

Hummingbirds enjoy bathing and in this area of their personal hygiene differ little from other birds. They bathe at least once daily, more frequently when the weather is hot and dry. They must, however, take their plunge on the wing and cannot, as other birds do, sit peacefully in the water and ruffle their wings. Sometimes they dive into pools of clear water, sometimes they flutter on small-leaved trees and shrubs wet with rain or dew, and when there is a small waterfall they fly through the falling droplets and enjoy a quick shower.

We come next to flight techniques and here, as noted earlier, we can be somewhat more categorical than in other areas. As with coloring, a more detailed discussion will be given in a later chapter. Hummingbird flight is different from that of any other bird, and the anatomy of their wings is unique. As I have said before, they are the only birds that can hover with body motionless. They are also the only ones that have a "reverse gear" which enables them to fly backwards as prettily and as efficiently as they can fly forwards.

Much has been written about the extremely rapid wing beat rate of hummingbirds, and in some cases it is indeed extremely high. A male *Calliphlox amethystina,* the subject of our dietary experiment a few paragraphs ago, beats its wings about 80 times per second, a rate much higher than anything recorded for what might be called an "ordinary" bird. *Calliphlox,* however, weighs only two and eight-tenths grams, and there is no ordinary bird so small. Since at the small end of the hummingbird scale we have no standard of reference, it cannot really be said whether the high wing beat rate is extraordinary or not.

For larger hummingbirds we can, however, begin to make comparisons. There are a great many of these whose wing beat rate is in the range of 20 to 25 per second, and whose weight would range between five and seven grams. By comparison a chickadee, one of the smallest of "ordinary" birds, flaps its wings about 27 times per second and is quite a bit larger (it weighs 12-13 grams) than any one of this group of hummingbirds. The largest hummingbird, *Patagona gigas,* beats its wings 8 to 10 times per second, a rate unusually low for a bird of its size. A mockingbird, by way of contrast, which is much larger, registers 14 beats per second.

North American hummingbirds have been more thoroughly studied than the others and since these are all small, with a correspondingly high wing beat rate, it is not surprising that the generalization has been made that all hummingbirds beat their wings with great rapidity. For the ruby throat, for example, the rate is about 50 per second for the female and 70 for the male. The difference, I might add, is not due to male superiority but simply to the fact that the female, for some reason which Nature doubtless considers good and sufficient, is, in this instance, the larger of the two.

I think it is safe to conclude that at a given wing length or weight hummingbirds beat their wings *less* rapidly than ordinary birds. The aerodynamic basis for this conclusion rests on the fact that while ordinary birds generate power only on the downbeat of their wings, hummingbirds get propulsion and lift during both downbeat and upbeat.

To accomplish their aerial gymnastics the hummingbird wing muscles, as one might expect, are very large and account for twenty-five

FOOD AND DRINK

Per unit of weight, the hummingbird expends the highest energy output of any warm-blooded animal, and its appetite is in proportion. In drinking, the long and adaptable tongue with its efficient pumping apparatus snakes forward like a length of fire hose. High speed photography now disproves an earlier notion that the bill itself had to contact the water—though the tongue is almost transparent, it is shown quite clearly foraging well ahead of the beak seeking out moisture for its needs.

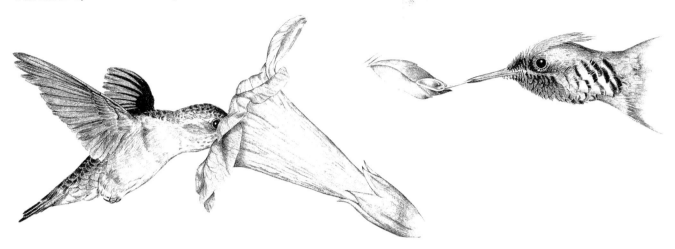

to thirty per cent of the weight of the entire bird. Here again I can make a human comparison. Since we use our legs to get about, perhaps the fair thing to do is to compare our leg muscles with the hummingbird's wing muscles. These for us average about sixteen per cent of our body weight; the hummingbird is about twice as well endowed.

Just as we have no wing muscles to speak of, and hence cannot fly, the hummingbird is equally deficient when it comes to getting about on its feet; it cannot walk at all in the ordinary sense. I have seen a bird sidle along on a perch, but even for the smallest distances it is far more apt to use wings than feet.

Finally, I must come, however reluctantly, to a serious deficiency in this otherwise striking family, and that is their vocal performance. In the sense in which our songbirds have a voice, hummingbirds have none at all. They do indeed chatter, particularly when they are annoyed and chasing each other, but the sound is scarcely musical. There are also

Patagona gigas

Calliphlox amethystina

LARGE AND SMALL

*Although many hummingbirds are small and the family in-
cludes the smallest bird known, the range is broad enough to
include the* Patagona gigas, *or "giant," an Andean species
as large as a bluebird or a swift. The tiny female* Calliphlox
amethystina *shown here is not the smallest hummingbird (a
distinction reserved for the Cuban* Calypte helenae) *but by
contrast is a third the* gigas' *length and a seventh its weight.*

records of courting sounds by groups of aspiring males of some species, but these are puny efforts indeed and can't begin to approach the musical offerings of even the poorest of our songbirds.

There seems rarely to be a generalization to which there are no exceptions. Having now demolished hummingbirds as songsters I must admit to one, with the improbable name *Schistes geoffroyi*, that has quite a decent song — nothing to make a thrush jealous — but to which an English sparrow, for example, might well aspire. So far as I am aware, among hummingbirds *Schistes* stands alone.

Nature, I suppose, must have its checks and balances, and no living animal, human beings not excepted, can be perfect in all particulars. Hummingbirds do manage and manage very well, and when it comes to courting I am not at all sure whether attracting a female with a sweet voice has any merit over a brilliant flash of color. In Nature's catalog, both seem to work.

The characteristics discussed thus far are more or less general for all of the three hundred and nineteen species. The variations encountered within the family, however, are very great. Color, size, shape of bill and tail vary over wide limits; more so, in fact, than in any other family of birds.

I have already mentioned the iridescent colors which quite literally cover the entire spectrum. Iridescent greens are predominant and if there is any color that is characteristic, that is it. There are, however, also reds, yellows, blues, purples, in all shades and in all intensities.

In most cases the male carries the iridescent color, usually in a patch of varying size on his throat. This iridescent gorget, as it is called, is sometimes small, equivalent perhaps to a circle three-eighths inch in diameter, and sometimes so large that the iridescent patch runs well down the chest and around both sides of the neck. In many cases there is also an iridescent crown most often a different color from that of the gorget. The belly is also quite frequently iridescent. Sometimes the

Eutoxeres aquila

Ensifera ensifera

BILLS

It is improbable that any family of related creatures varies so widely in physical equipment as do the hummingbirds. The Alpha and Omega of their bill range are represented by the Ensifera *with its great sword-like beak and* Ramphomicron microrhynchum, *whose name translates rather redundantly as "small bill small bill." The extremes differ by a factor of about one to twelve. The "sickle bill," above, is unique unto itself.*

Ramphomicron microrhynchum ♀

brilliant coloration is found on the tail and tail coverts and in rarer cases on the back. Nature has also arranged matters so that the admiring female can see the iridescence on whatever part of the body it may be and the male, when he is disposed to go courting, can present himself to full advantage.

As already noted, the birds in general are quite tiny. Unfortunately weights have been recorded for only a few species. The eastern ruby throat weighs a little over three grams, or about one hundred and fifty birds to the pound, and is neither the smallest nor the largest hummingbird. The little *Calypte helenae* might weigh as little as two grams, and the largest of the family, *Patagona gigas,* about twenty.

The bill is perhaps the most variable feature in the family. It ranges in length from the extraordinary five-inch bill of *Ensifera ensifera* to the tiny protuberance of *Rhamphomicron microrhynchum.* (An example of ornithological tautology—*Rhamphomicron* and *microrhynchum* both mean "little bill.") Some are modestly curved downwards; one or two curved upwards. And there is the extraordinary *Eutoxeres,* whose common name is, for obvious reasons, sickle bill.

The tail also is quite variable. The winner for tail length is probably the Jamaican streamer tail, and there are all ranges between its two long pennants and what one might call a reasonable norm. There are also special variations: the racket tails, for example, which carry little flags at the end of a fairly long quill.

The most unusual of the racket tails is *Loddigesia mirabilis* from Peru who when courting flies back and forth before his mate with his two rackets raised to frame his face, a maneuver which he obviously thinks renders him doubly enchanting.

There are other decorative appendages of great variety. Some birds have beards, some crests, some both; some extensible collars with iridescent terminations. This shows, I suppose, the lengths to which a male will go to make himself attractive to a female. Whether it is preferable to our reverse system is a question I will leave to philosophers.

The females, as I have indicated, are quite uniformly unspectacular. The rule in general is that the male is the gay one, though in many cases he too is unpretentious, at least as to coloring. As is general with most birds, promiscuity is more certain to occur when the male is gay than when he is drab. Apparently in the latter case he has nothing to rely upon but an approximation to marital fidelity.

Finally we come to a discussion of hummingbird behavior. I should say at once that behavior in an ornithological sense does not concern itself with good table manners or speaking respectfully to elders. Ornithologically speaking, behavior means the manner in which birds meet the major crises of their lives. In human terms, and here the analogy is very close, we would speak of adolescence, maturity, courtship, marriage, and the rearing of young.

In their day-to-day living the outstanding characteristics of hummingbirds are their fearlessness, pugnacity, and curiosity. They seem fully aware of their unusual aerial capabilities and understand that they can sense danger and get away much more rapidly than larger, slower moving enemies can move in to the attack.

We see this in their almost complete disregard for the presence of humans; even in the wilderness a hummingbird will approach to within five or ten feet. In more civilized surroundings they become so used to people that they will feed from the hand, and I have even seen them perch on a finger held closely in front of their feeding station. This is not at all because they have love and affection for humanity. It is a reflection only of complete confidence in their ability to make a fast getaway should anything untoward happen.

They are said to be attracted by anything that is bright red in color, although this has been disputed by some observers. My own experience is that red is indeed their favorite. I have seen them on many occasions explore the red plastic knobs of my camera tripod, and on one

BELLIGERENCE

Though often outweighed by opponents, humming-birds are courageous and aggressive battlers. A hummingbird in defense of his territorial bound-aries will attack a catbird with impunity and has been known to engage a hawk a hundred times his size, diving at his adversary with well-aimed thrusts of his sharp beak. Among themselves they are equally touchy and when feeding will drive off any rival who dares venture near enough to compete.

Calypte anna

occasion when I was rash enough to be wearing a red tie they prodded at it, doubtless to see whether it contained anything good to eat. When we were photographing caged birds in Ecuador, someone had hung a thermometer filled with red alcohol on the wall of the cage and each of the hummingbirds in turn tested this out for nutritional value.

Like most other birds they establish territories which they defend vigorously whether or not the intruder is of their own family and quite regardless of size. A hummingbird will chivvy a catbird, routing him quite successfully from the territorial boundaries. I have, however, a rather deep suspicion that all hummingbirds have a touch of the Irish in them, for their belligerence goes far beyond the simple needs of terri-torial defense. I would be quite certain that they engage in their aerial jousts more for the fun of it than for any other reason.

A group of well-attended feeders in a garden is a never-ending source of delight. A particular hummingbird will take possession of a given feeder, driving off all comers. This process goes on endlessly, first one bird and then the other winning out in their battles, all of this accompanied by a continuous stream of indignant chatter.

When it comes to courtship and "marriage" I am afraid I can tell no tales of marital fidelity and "growing old together." Each male is a feathered Don Juan with interests limited to food, fighting, and courtship. His courtship display is a veritable aerial circus. I have seen it myself for only a few species but the literature seems to say that all males behave in much the same way. The female ruby throat settles herself on a twig fairly near the ground. The male rises high in the air and launches a power dive which ends immediately in front of his dazzled mate-to-be, then rises precipitously so that his course resembles a large U with the female at its base. In this performance she chooses her position (or he chooses it for her) in such a way that she sees the light reflected from all of his iridescent parts and so has the joy not only of his aerial acrobatics but of a beautiful color display as well. If she succumbs, he dashes off to other conquests, leaving her to deal, alone and unaided, with the consequences of their union.

When the males are dull colored they appear to rely on other ways of charming their ladies. Here for example is Dr. Augusto Ruschi's description of the courtship of *Phaethornis ruber*—

> "The male flies in circles very near the female, above and around her, chirping low as she watches him, turning her head to follow his movements. He approaches more closely and opening his bill sticks out his tongue and lets it drop in an exquisite and ridiculous manner . . . until the female at last gives signs of potential surrender."

Need I repeat after all this that hummingbirds are largely polygamous and promiscuous? The males, in fact, do not invariably insist on females of their own species. The considerable number of hybrids that have been identified bears witness to that fact.

Leaving the male to his philandering, the female who has been courted and won proceeds immediately to her nest-building with apparently no thought (aside from a casual battle or two) for anything except the procreation of her race.

The hummingbirds are without question among the most accomplished avian architects. The tiny nests are much alike, beautifully and carefully fashioned. Fine down lines the inner cup in which the eggs are laid. Coarser material is used for the outer layers, and the final exterior decoration consists of small bits of lichen that provide both camouflage and beauty. As reinforcement, stolen spider webbing is invariably used, and this serves not only to hold the nest together but to attach it securely to the twig which supports it. The effect when completed is lovely and the assiduous mother will go on decorating and redecorating even after the eggs are laid and incubation has started.

One notable exception in outward appearance is the nest of the genus *Phaethornis*.* Many of this genus hang their nests from some suitable support using a ribbon of vegetation reinforced with long fibers or spider webbing attached only to one side of the nest. Such a structure, which has the general form of an inverted cone, obviously needs counterbalancing if the bird is to sit in comfort without being tipped out. This is accomplished by weaving into the bottom of the cone lumps of dirt which in effect counterbalance the weight of the bird in the nest and keep the top surface horizontal.

Another exception, and as far as I know the only other, is the nests of the genera *Glaucis* and *Rhamphodon*. These are like *Phaethornis* nests in shape but are fashioned entirely of fine fern roots, so insubstantially put together that one can actually see the eggs through the sides of the nest.

The egg quota of a hummingbird is almost invariably two, and the incubation period of the order of twelve to sixteen days. In nest building, as well as in incubation, the females are unusually fearless. I have had camera, flash lamps, and self within four feet of a nest under

*These birds vary in size but are alike in the sense that they are dull colored, having no iridescence, but with extremely elegant tails, the middle two feathers prolonged into dashing streamers.

construction and the lady went on building, paying no more attention to me or my equipment than if I were merely a part of the scenery.

During incubation also I have had my head within a few feet of a sitting bird. All she did was to give me one of those quizzical looks that warned me of dire things to happen if I came any closer.

Eventually the young hatch and the feeding process begins. This is a fearsome sight. The mother arrives at the side of the nest, the young stretch out their gaping mouths, whereupon she inserts her bill to a depth that makes one certain it will come through on the other side, and literally pumps nourishment into the young one. The longer the bill the more terrifying the process. I have never seen the sword bill in action but I should think that would be a sight to shock the hardiest soul. The process, however, seems to work, for there is no record, in the literature or out, of a young one being impaled by an overassiduous mother.

The time the young are in the nest is quite variable, much more so than for most small birds. In the case of the ruby throat, for which there is an abundance of data, the nestling period varies from as little as ten to as much as thirty days and the frequency of food delivery by the mother is in inverse proportion.

In the one or two cases I have been able to observe at firsthand, there seems to be no correlation of nestling period with either temperature or time of year. I have a theory to account for this variation but I hasten to say that it is no more than a theory and I have no facts to affirm or deny.

As I noted earlier, however, an adult bird leading a reasonably active life must take on a supply of fuel every ten or fifteen minutes. When there are young on the nest the female has the added burden of collecting enough insects and nectar to keep her young happy and growing. If she happens to choose a site for her nest far removed from flowers, which are her own source of energy, it is obvious that the margin of time she has to collect insects for the young decreases.

NESTS

No bird excels the female hummingbird in the elegance and structural suitability of nest architecture. The cone-shaped type at the left is delicately counterbalanced to keep it steady. Those at the right are more representative of the norm. All employ some degree of exterior decoration, the outside being enriched with bits of lichen. Stolen spider webbing is invariably used as reinforcement and for a secure mooring to the chosen nesting place.

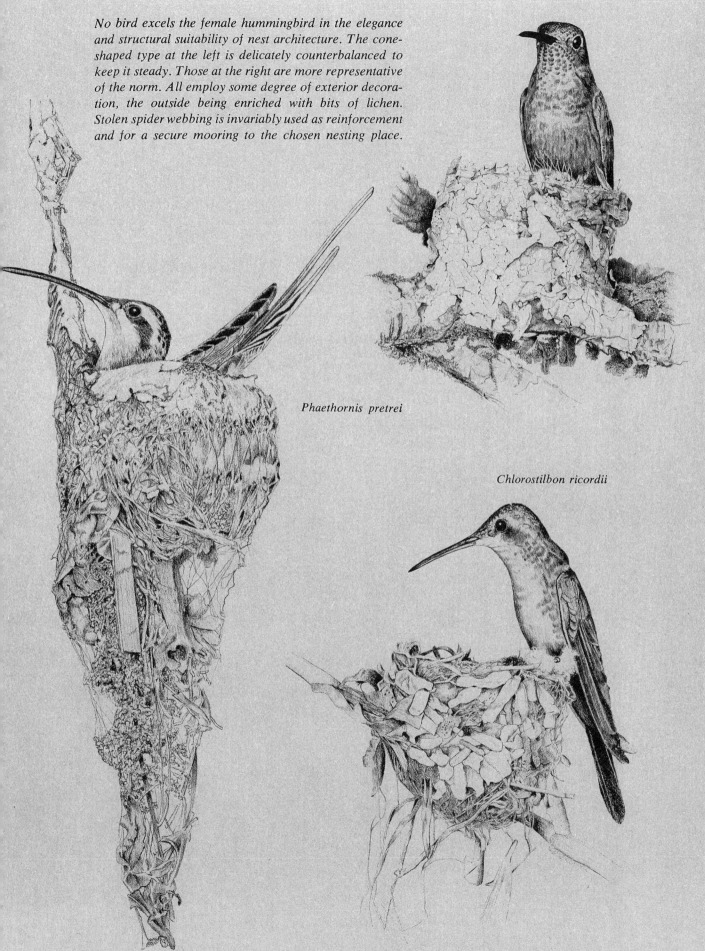

Archilochus colubris

Phaethornis pretrei

Chlorostilbon ricordii

It would seem that the rate at which the mother can raise her young must depend upon the availability of fuel for herself. If flowers are far distant from her nesting site, she will be able to feed her young only at long intervals. If her own food is close at hand she will be able to do correspondingly better. Perhaps since adults have the ability to decrease their metabolic rate the young can also, and so survive the longer period between feedings.

The young, whatever their sex, when they leave the nest and for some time thereafter, resemble the female, and the males do not acquire their full resplendent iridescence until after their first molt, about a year after they have hatched.

And here again family ties are soon broken and when the young are old enough to fend for themselves they become individuals in their own right and are quite as likely to do battle with their mothers as they are with young from a neighboring nest.

Here then are the hummingbirds—striking little creatures, gay, fearless, pugnacious, and colorful. Perhaps, after all, the Comte de Buffon did not exaggerate, and nature did indeed "load them with all the gifts of which she has only given other birds a share."

FEEDING THE YOUNG

The female hummingbird is a dedicated mother and homemaker. She lays two eggs which hatch in a fortnight or so and for the next three weeks she attends her charges devotedly. Feeding is an awesome spectacle. Probing deeply with her beak into the throats of the young, she pumps in a regurgitated formula in a series of convulsive thrusts. Before venturing flight, several days are spent in exercising the wings of the fledglings.

chapter 2

FEATHERS, COLOR AND IRIDESCENCE

In versatility and elegance, Nature's creative effort provides a never-ending source of astonishment and delight. She is tireless and imaginative in her innovations. Having evolved a happy solution to a given problem, it might be expected that she would rest content, adopting her discovery universally. Instead, she seems determined to demonstrate that the same problem can be solved, and solved brilliantly, in many ways and always with a great show of virtuosity.

The outer coverings Nature has devised for the protection of her various creatures afford an excellent case in point. Dogs and cats and lions and bears, for example, are clothed in fur, as are monkeys and ocelots. Fish have scales. Turtles and armadillos face life from the security of hard shells fastened firmly to their bodies, as do clams and oysters and abalones. Lobsters and shrimp, crickets and grasshoppers also have hard outer coverings—theirs less like traveling fortresses than delicate and beautifully fitted suits of armor.

We humans have allowed the fur which once came as standard equipment to atrophy and, using the intelligence which sets us off from other creatures, have devised substitutes. Thus, we have our nylons and cottons and woolens, our shorts and sweaters and slacks, garb for evening and garb for day. Rather pretentiously, we attach significance to their style and cut, and even to the labels they bear, as with Dior frocks and Brooks Brothers shirts. Whether the result does our intellect credit is debatable. We have achieved variety, to be sure, but functionally, I doubt that we have improved very much upon our original furry coverall. Nature is a master designer and is hard to best.

It is footless, I suppose, to attempt a judgment as to the relative merits of Nature's accomplishments in the field of animal haberdashery. Each seems to serve its purpose and that, after all, is the only proper criterion by which inventive genius should be appraised. It is my own opinion, however, delivered in an appropriately small voice, that in outfitting her various charges, Mother Nature has reserved her most ingenious and satisfactory solution for the class Aves.

In the design of the feather Nature really outdid herself. Basically, a feather is a simple structure consisting of shaft, barbs and barbules. Yet these three elements are combined so imaginatively that they take shape as wings for flight, as tails for braking, steering, and maneuvering and as body cover for insulation and streamlining, forming, as well, a variety of crests, beards, and other appendages of uncertain functional value. Such refinements as water repellency have been added when necessary for aquatic pursuits and, in the interest of procreation, males are usually provided with a range of gorgeous colors irresistible to prospective mates. The result is an animal of extraordinary resource, capable of making its home in tropic heat or Arctic cold, in forest or meadow, on desert or mountain, equipped to withstand rain or snow, harsh winds or burning sun, eluding its ground-fast enemies with ease and grace. A remarkable creature, an astonishing conception.

The structural technique represented in these many specialized feathers is in itself a fascinating study. Shape and alignment of shaft, barb and barbule have been varied to produce not only the desired form, but to give the special characteristics required: strength where needed, flexibility elsewhere. Many of man's contrivances have been anticipated. A zipper-like link between adjacent barbs permits them to part under stress, yet resume their original form when pressures recede. Much has been written on feather structure; so much, in fact, that even the shortest of summaries would add unconscionable length to this account.

The feathering of hummingbirds at first glance would appear relatively sparse. Dr. Alexander Wetmore once undertook the tedious task of counting feathers and reported that the ruby throated humming-bird has 940 as compared, for example, with 1,960 for a brown thrasher and 8,325 for a Plymouth Rock. When one considers feathers per unit area, however, the relationships are quite different. The brown thrasher, for example, has a surface area about ten times that of the ruby throat, with only twice the number of feathers. Per unit of body surface, one sees that the ruby throat bests the thrasher by a factor of five. In fact, hummingbirds may well be more closely feathered than any other family.

The hummingbird's functional feathers do not differ greatly from those of other birds. Their body plumage in most particulars is much like that of sparrows and hawks and ducks. Tail and wing feathers show only small structural differences adapting them to the hummingbird's unusual maneuverability and method of flight.

The hummingbird feathers which are unique and which have no counterpart in the entire avian population are those which produce the iridescent colors characteristic of the family. Nature has bestowed upon the hummingbird a dazzling burst of color, yet, like a prudent mother concerned lest her children engage in immodest excesses, she carefully restricts the range of display. The feathers not only carry the sub-microscopic structures which produce the color, but their component parts are

These pictures of a male Chrysolampis mosquitus *show how the position of the bird controls the brilliance of the iridescent colors as recorded by the camera.*

[These photos appear in color on last page of color insert.]

so arranged that it can be seen only within a narrowly defined set of positions involving the bird, the sun and the observer. When all three are in their proper places, the color shines out in all its resplendent brilliance, but if the positions change even a trifle the bird looks drab and dark.

A feather from the iridescent gorget of a hummingbird has first of all a shaft which penetrates the skin and forms the point of attachment to the body of the bird. Near the skin the shaft carries uncolored, thread-like barbs extending out from either side, providing an insulating layer which protects the bird's tender skin from the elements. As we move out along the shaft the function of the barbs undergoes a change and with it the structure, until finally at the tip of the feather they show the characteristic color in all its glory.

The feathers lie one on top of the other, much like shingles on a roof. Only the brightly colored tip is visible; the uncolored insulating portions are hidden by adjacent feathers. The analogy with shingles still holds—one-third of the length of a particular feather shows, the rest of it lies under the overlap of its neighbors.

In describing the structure of these iridescent barbs, I confess to great mental anguish in finding words which can clarify, even for an attentive reader, this beautifully complex exercise in three-dimensional geometry. Someone has said that the most difficult forensic assignment conceivable is to describe a shoe to a man who has never seen one. My task, I think, is even more demanding; it is rather like an intelligent horse trying to describe to equine associates who had never seen a man the shape, structure and utility of a human hand.

Whatever our intelligent horse would do (perhaps he would do better than I) I have given up, after many tries, on a proper description of the iridescent feather as it is. In what follows, I attempt to indicate, instead, how something similar might be constructed in the hope that it will be more readily understandable than a necessarily inadequate description of the finished product.

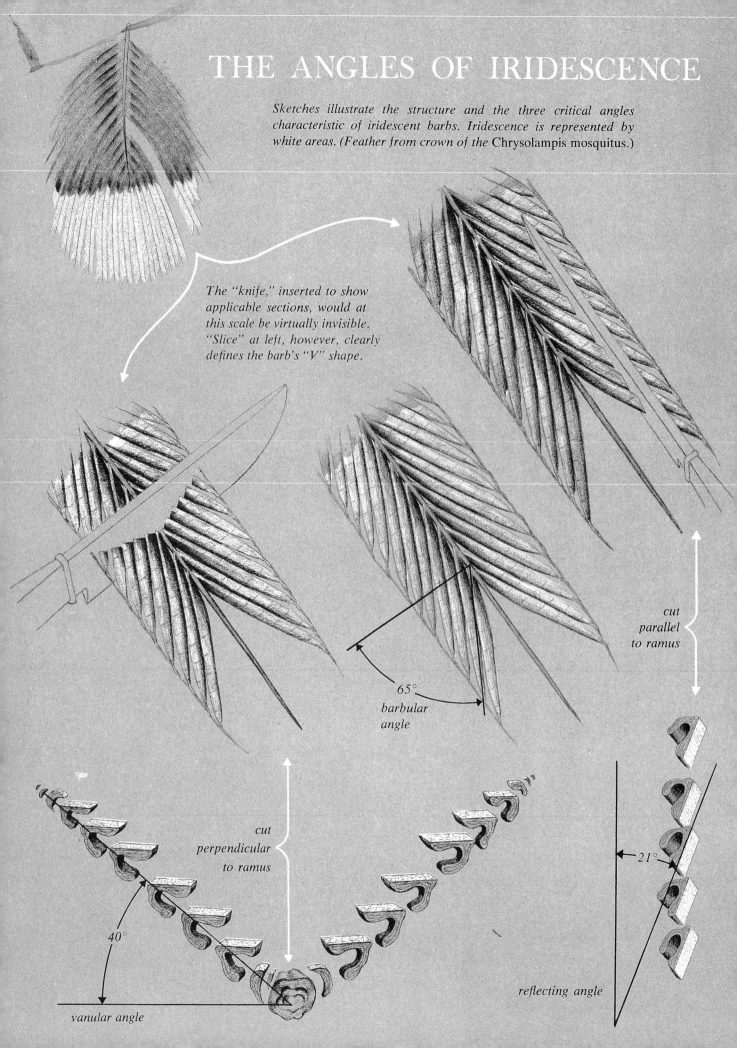

THE ANGLES OF IRIDESCENCE

Sketches illustrate the structure and the three critical angles characteristic of iridescent barbs. Iridescence is represented by white areas. (Feather from crown of the Chrysolampis mosquitus.)

The "knife," inserted to show applicable sections, would at this scale be virtually invisible. "Slice" at left, however, clearly defines the barb's "V" shape.

65°
barbular
angle

cut
parallel
to ramus

cut
perpendicular
to ramus

40°

vanular angle

21°

reflecting angle

Suppose, then, that we take a wooden pole a few inches in diameter and, for the sake of rigidity, fasten it to a small table in such a way that it bisects the surface. We now find two sections of venetian blind, perhaps 18 inches wide. After rounding off the four corners of each slat and making the slats reflecting by gluing to the top surface of each a strip of polished aluminum foil, we lay these on the table on either side of the pole, making sure that pairs of slats on each side are in a straight line, like ribs on a spinal column. Let us now fasten the ends of the slats flexibly to the pole by using, for example, screw eyes in the pole and hooks in the slats.

We now take two long strips of wood—laths will do—and lay them endwise along the outer edges of the venetian blind. The outer end of each slat is then fastened flexibly to the laths, just as its inner end was fastened to the pole.

With slats secured to pole and lath, we pull the laths toward us, sliding them along on the table surface until the slats are at an angle to the axis of the pole, the assembly now resembling the chevrons on a top sergeant's sleeve.

Next, we grasp both laths and lift them vertically so that each row of slats forms an angle with the surface of the table. By kneeling and looking at the structure endwise, one should see a V-shaped trough.

As the final act, we take the piece of cord which adjusts the angles of the slats of a venetian blind and pull it so that the reflecting surfaces turn away from us. We adjust the angle until the sun, shining from the other side of the table and in a vertical plane which includes the axis of the pole, is reflected to our eye from each of the reflecting slats. We should now be looking at a greatly enlarged model of the barb of an iridescent hummingbird feather.

To go from model-making to ornithology, it now becomes necessary to supply the proper names of the various components of the structure just completed.

The entire assembly is called a *barb*.
The pole is the *ramus*.
The two venetian blinds are the *vanules*.
The individual slats are the *barbules*.
The lath represents a structural element made up of the terminal
parts of the barbules, called the *pennula* (singular: *pennulum*),
each of which nests neatly into its neighbor.

There are, of course, no hooks and eyes in nature and the barbules (slats) grow out of the ramus (pole) in the right direction and at the proper angles. Nor do the laths exist in nature. Each barbule (slat) terminates in a pennulum which grows out of the barbule in a direction parallel to the ramus (pole). Each pennulum is equipped with little spines or hooklets so that a row of pennula, nested into each other, will hold the structure together quite as well as the lath in our model.

We see from our model-making exercise that there are three critical angles. The first of these is the angle that the individual barbules (slats) make with a perpendicular to the ramus (pole), measured as a projection on the surface of the table. This we call the barbular angle. The second is the angle that the two vanules (venetian blinds) make with the table. This we call the vanular angle. The third angle is contained between a ruler laid across the reflecting surface of each barbule, or slat (parallel to the ramus, or pole), with the surface of the table. This we call the reflecting angle.

To complete the structure in a way such that light shining along the trough of the barb will reflect directly upward to the eye, the three angles must have a precise relationship to each other. That relationship requires that the tangent of the vanular angle, divided by the tangent of the barbular angle, equal the tangent of the reflecting angle.

This simple formula shows many possible combinations of vanular and barbular angles for a given reflecting angle. The barbular angles, for example, will vary from zero to $70°$, vanular angles from zero to $45°$,

and reflecting angles from zero to $45°$.

The effect of variations in these angles on what one sees is about as follows: The smaller the vanular angle; i.e., the more nearly the two vanules lie in the same plane, the less critical the position of bird, sun and observer. The color of the bird is brilliantly visible from many positions. The value for the reflecting angle will depend largely upon the location of the iridescent areas. The gorget, for example, is nearly vertical when the bird is perched, and the reflecting angle for these feathers must be small to permit the color to be seen at eye level. The abdomen, on the other hand, is more nearly horizontal, and the reflecting angle must increase if both abdomen and gorget are to show their colors simultaneously. (Eye level in this sense does not refer to a human observer, but to the eye of the prospective mate which the male is attempting to impress.)

I must now confess to having cheated a little in depicting the barbule as if it were a slat of a venetian blind. Actually only its top surface is slat-like; there is also a lower surface provided presumably for structural reinforcement. We can produce something like the actual barbule by taking a strip of sheet aluminum and folding it along its length to produce a shape which in cross section resembles a V turned on its side. The top surface is the slat of our model; the lower surface appears to act principally as a stiffener. Where the barbule undergoes its transition to the pennulum, the cross section changes from a V to, let us say,

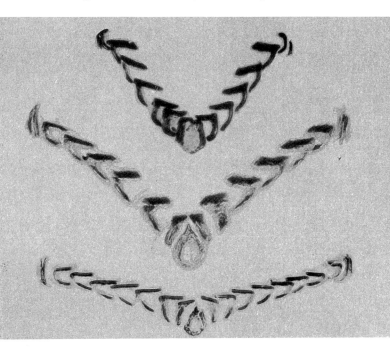

HOW ANGLES VARY

Vanular angles vary over wide limits. Here are photomicrographs of cross sections through barbs from top, a crown feather from Chrysolampis mosquitus, *center, a chest feather from* Boissonneaua jardini *and at bottom, a crown feather from* Aglaieocercus kingi.

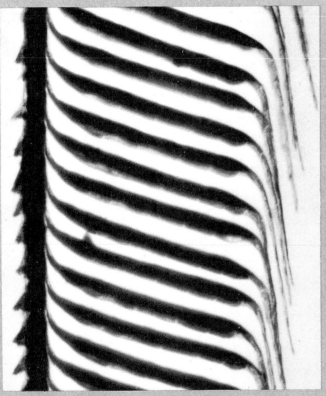

MORPHOLOGY

Here are presented a collection of photomicrographs at a magnification of about 300x. At the top is the tip of an iridescent barb (bright green) from the crown of Aglaiocercus kingi. At left, center, is a segment of a barb (brilliant blue green) from the chest of Boissonneaua jardini. Pressure on the segment has caused the pennula to spread, showing more clearly their positional relationship to the barbule and to each other. Below is a group of pennula showing how these can vary in shape and in the design of the associated hooklets. Left to right 1, 2) Chrysolampis mosquitus—crown, two sides of barb, 3) Heliangelus viola—gorget, 4) Chrysolampis mosquitus—gorget, 5) Aglaiocercus kingi—tail. The large spines here are to take care of the heavy extra pressures to which tail feathers, by virtue of function, are subject.

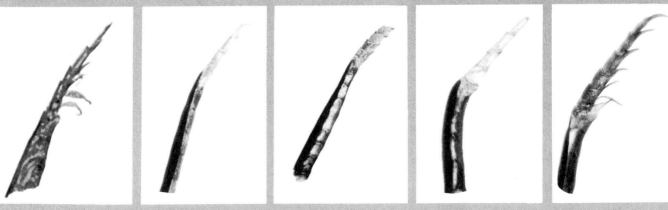

one side of a parenthesis, [( ]. From here on, as the pennulum takes its position parallel to the ramus, it tapers down to a point. Adjacent pennula nest into each other [((( ], to give rigidity to the entire structure.

The model we constructed of the iridescent barb, using poles, laths and venetian blinds, was enormously larger than life-size. To speak conveniently of actual dimensions in this microscopic area, we require a unit of length less cumbersome than inches. For such purposes physicists use the "micron," which is 1/1000 of a millimeter and approximately 1/25,000 of an inch. Using these as our unit, the total width of the barb is about 200 microns, the length of an individual barbule is 100 microns, and its width about 15 microns. It would take about 125 barbs laid side by side to measure an inch. Similarly, if we took 425,000 barbules and arranged them in 250 adjacent rows of 1,700 barbules each, we would have an area about one inch on each side. The detail of an entire barb is barely visible to the naked eye. Individual barbules can be seen only with the aid of the microscope.

These tiny structures are designed in the best engineering tradition. The ramus is tubular for maximum stiffness and minimum weight. The V-shaped barbular cross section insures proper placement of the reflecting surface. The nested pennula with their zipper-like fasteners combine rigidity and flexibility. The whole barb is unbelievably light yet adequately strong. Nature's craftsmanship is superb, as always.

So far we have spoken only of the brilliant iridescent feathers which exist principally to catch the eye of a potential mate. Even though this account may be unduly prolonged, I cannot resist adding a brief description of the feathers clothing the remainder of the bird's body.

These feathers also are iridescent, the color with few exceptions a yellowish green. Here, however, the color can be seen from all viewpoints; the directional effect characteristic of gorget feathers is absent. The colors also are much less brilliant. Both differences come about because of a radical modification of the structure of the barbule.

BACK FEATHER

An iridescent barb (rose red) from the back of Aglaeactis cupripennis (Plate 26). A cross section through a barbule resembles a semicircle with its ends pointing upward. As a result of this, iridescence may be seen from all directions.

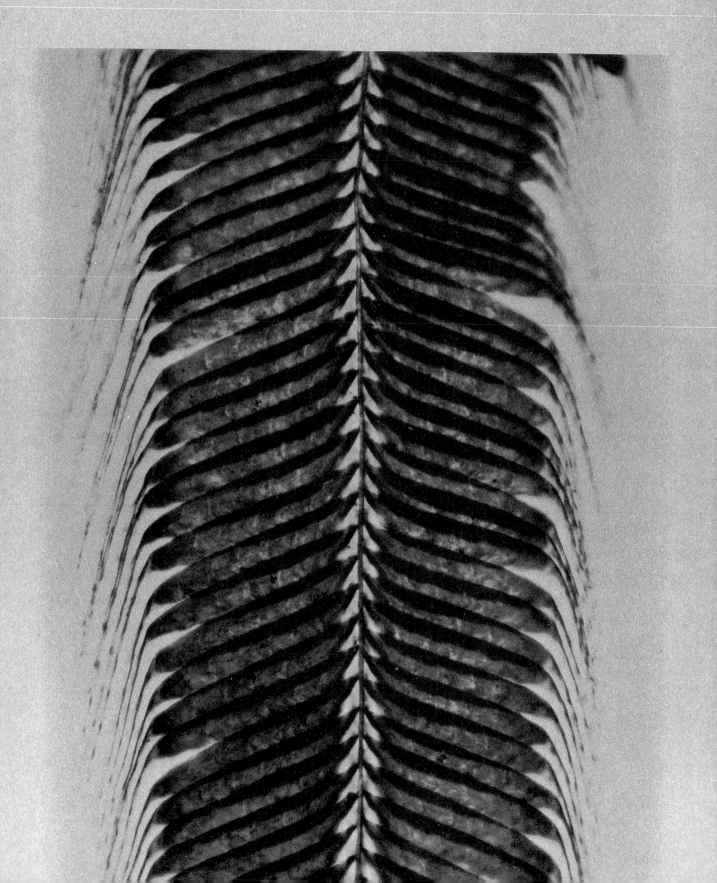

The gorget barbules have a cross section resembling a V laid on its side, the perfectly flat top behaving like a tiny mirror reflecting light in one direction only. In the back feathers the cross section resembles a semicircle with the ends pointing upward: ⌣, forming in effect a curved mirror. For light coming from whatever direction, some portion will be reflected to the viewer wherever he may be with respect to illuminant and bird. Of course, only a small segment of the curved mirror comes into play for any given angle of observation, hence the color will appear far less brilliant than would be seen if the mirror surface were flat and all of the reflected light concentrated toward a given point.

The gorget, as has been noted, is quite dark and dull when illuminant, bird and observer are out of their proper relationship. I suppose Nature could not tolerate this condition for the whole bird and arranged matters so that some color would be evident whatever the bird's position with respect to the observer.

So much for geometry and feather structure. We should now be turning to the submicroscopic elements which produce the color. Before discussing them, it may be as well to say something about the physics of light and color.

Light coming to us from the sun is a mixture of many colors to which our human eyes are so attuned that we have the impression of white or uncolored light. This was beautifully demonstrated by Sir Isaac Newton 250 years ago. In Newton's experiment, a narrow beam of sunlight was directed on one face of a prism which dispersed the incoming beam into its basic spectral colors. The dispersed beam in turn was made to fall on a second pair of prisms and on passing through these prisms, the dispersed elements recombined into the original beam of white light.

The sensation of a particular color is, therefore, produced by subtracting the unwanted components from white light. A blue dress, for example, looks blue because the red and green components of white

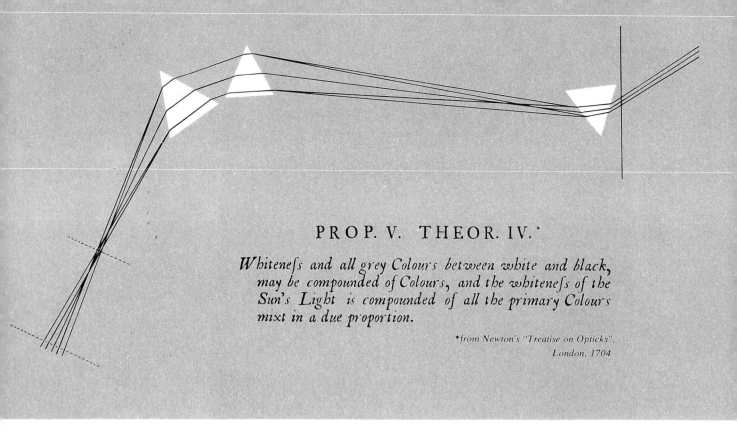

PROP. V. THEOR. IV. *

Whitenefs and all grey Colours between white and black, may be compounded of Colours, and the whitenefs of the Sun's Light is compounded of all the primary Colours mixt in a due proportion.

*from Newton's "Treatise on Opticks", London, 1704

light are destroyed or absorbed and only the blue component is reflected. A leaf is green because its surface absorbs the red and blue components, reflecting only the green.

Most of the colors we see result from selective light absorption by chemical compounds which we call dyes or pigments, whose molecules are so constructed that certain colors are absorbed while others are reflected. In nature, the green of grass and foliage, the infinite variety in the colors of flowers, the red of a ruby, even the red-brown of fresh earth, all are caused by the presence of some naturally occurring chemical substance which absorbs certain colors into itself while reflecting others. The synthesis of dyestuffs and pigments in an infinite variety of shades and hues, making color an inexpensive commonplace, is one of the triumphs of modern chemistry.

Colors are characterized by their wave lengths. The situation is quite closely analogous to what happens when a pebble is tossed into a still pool of water. A circular wave front extends outward from the disturbance caused by the pebble. If one imagines a continuous disturbance starting at a given point, such as might be caused by a steady stream

40

of pebbles, the ripples on the pool would extend out continuously until reflected from the edge of the pool or absorbed on, let us say, a sandy beach. The distance from the crest of one wave to that of its neighbor is the "wave length" of the ripple.

In just this way, a light source sends out a continuous wave front which travels on through space until it is reflected or absorbed. The wave length is shortest for blue, longest for red, the ratio of the two being roughly as two is to three.

Colors can also be produced by purely physical as distinct from chemical structures. The molecular linkages in dyestuffs and pigments operate invariably by the absorption or destruction of the unwanted colors. For the color producing physical structures, on the other hand, color appears because undesired components of white light have merely been diverted out of our line of sight.

The most common physical or structural color is the blue of the sky. Sunlight comes through space as an uninterrupted beam. When the light approaches the earth, it meets the resistance of submicroscopic particles which are present in great abundance in the atmosphere. The light of the longer wave lengths passes through these particles virtually unchanged. The blue light, being of shorter wave length, is partially deflected or scattered by these particles and, bouncing from one to another, appears to reach us from all directions. This is why the sky looks blue. The point here is that the chemical nature of the scattering particles is of no significance. It is only their size which counts.

Prisms such as Newton used in his classical experiment can also produce structural colors through a property of light called refraction. Rays of light are bent, or refracted, as they pass from one substance, air for example, into another, such as glass. Refraction results from the fact that the speed of light is not constant, but depends on the nature of the substance through which the light is passing. The ratio of the speed of light in air to its speed in the substance in question is called

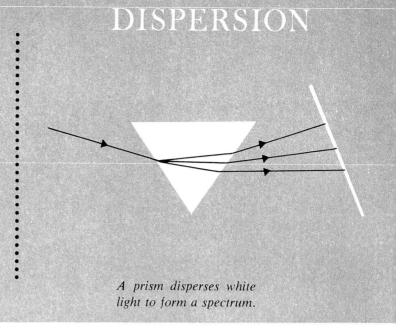

Light rays are bent as they pass from air into a glass plate and out again.

A prism disperses white light to form a spectrum.

the refractive index of the substance. Water, for example, has a refractive index of 1.33 which means simply that the speed of light in air is 1.33 times its speed in water. Glass has a refractive index of about 1.5, a diamond an index of 2.4.

A beam of light entering a substance of higher refractive index is always bent in such a way that the angle of refraction is less than the angle of incidence.* The reverse is true when the beam enters a substance of lower refractive index.

The refractive index differs very slightly with the color or wave length of the light. The bending of the light ray is most for blue light, least for red. This is why light emerging from a face of Newton's prism is no longer white, but has been decomposed into a brilliant spectrum of colors—violet, blue, green, yellow, orange and red. Red light is deviated least from its original direction and violet light most. The colors are exactly those we see in a rainbow and they occur in the same order.

A rainbow, the flash of colored light from a diamond, or from the beveled edge of plate glass, all arise because an incoming beam of light is refracted and dispersed into its component colors.

The type of structural color with which we are primarily concerned here is the result of the phenomenon called interference. Interference colors are familiar; the colors in a soap bubble, for example, or those we see in a film of oil on a wet asphalt pavement.

*The angle of incidence is the angle between the incoming beam and a perpendicular to the surface on which the beam falls.

To get an idea of the origin of interference colors, let us go back to the pebbles tossed into a still pool. If we could contrive matters in such a way that two pebbles were thrown into the pool at intervals such that the two wave fronts differed in phase by precisely one-half wave length, then the trough of one wave would coincide with the crest of the second. The effect would be one of mutual destruction and there would be no wave front at all. If, on the other hand, the two pebbles struck the surface exactly one wave length apart, troughs and crests would coincide and the resulting wave would have twice the intensity of either wave taken alone.

The problem now is to transfer our scene of action from ripples in a pond to light beams.

When a light beam passes from a material of one refractive index to another, the greater part of the light is refracted or bent in passing through the substance, as we showed a few paragraphs ago. In addition, a small portion of the incident light beam is reflected just as it would be from a mirror.

This again is something we see regularly. If we are in a brightly lighted room at night and look at the window, we see in the window-

CRESTS AND TROUGHS

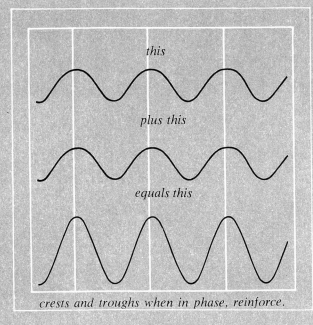

this

plus this

equals this

crests and troughs when in phase, reinforce.

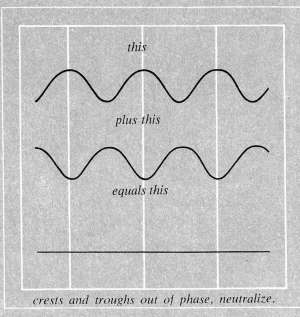

this

plus this

equals this

crests and troughs out of phase, neutralize.

pane a reflection of the room. If we look carefully, we can see a double reflection. The first reflection arises from the air-glass surface inside the room, the second from the glass-air surface on the outdoor side of the window. The percentage of the incident light which is reflected is small—about 4 per cent for a single glass-air interface. This is why we see no reflection during the day. The light coming in from outside simply overwhelms the small amount which is reflected from within.

The percentage of the incident beam which is reflected increases with the difference between the refractive indices of the two media. For glass and air (refractive indices 1.5 and 1.0), the reflectance is 4 per cent for each surface; 8 per cent for the two sides of a pane of glass. For a diamond (refractive index 2.4, one of the highest for any substance) in air the reflectance from two surfaces is 34 per cent. The high reflectance of the diamond can present problems, quite theoretical for most of us. I once saw a lady's wrist watch to which a diamond crystal had been fitted. The surface reflectance was so high that it became quite difficult to tell the time. I'm sure this proves something, perhaps only that it is unwise to depart too far from functionality, and that a diamond, like the shoemaker, had better stick to its last.

We can now begin to glimpse the mechanism by which interference in light beams is brought about. Imagine a very thin film with a higher refractive index than air. This we can produce by dipping a small wire hoop into a soap-water mixture. Light falling on the soap film will be partially reflected from both the front and rear surfaces. Because the speed of light is less within the soap film and the path longer, the train of light waves reflected from the back surface will be retarded or delayed with respect to the train reflected from the front surface. To make matters simpler, let us assume that we are dealing with a light beam of a single color, say blue. If now the thickness of the soap film is so adjusted that the retardation of the second beam with respect to the first is exactly half the wave length of blue light, then the two beams will neutralize each other and the bubble will look black. If, on the other hand, the thickness is adjusted so that the second beam is retarded by a full wave length, then crests and troughs will coincide and the reflected light will be more intensely blue than we would see from either surface.

We simplified matters somewhat by assuming a soap film of constant thickness and light of a single pure color. Our actual soap film varies in thickness as the soap-water solution drains to the bottom of the hoop, and light, of course, is made up of colors of all wave lengths. What we actually see is a color spectrum ranging from top to bottom of the soap film since the steadily increasing thickness of the film will eliminate first the blue component, then the green, and finally the red.

As we look at an actual soap film which has been given time to drain from top to bottom, we see a black band at the top extending down some distance before colors begin to appear. At first sight, this would seem to deny our theory since one might expect for this very thin part of the soap film that the two beams would be nearly in phase and, therefore, the net reflectance should be substantial rather than virtually nonexistent. It happens, however, that light waves reflected in passing from a medium of lower to one of higher refractive index (air to soap film in our case) turn upside down, or reverse their phase. Hence, the more nearly our soap film approaches zero thickness, the more nearly the two reflected beams will be out of phase such as to neutralize each other.

It follows also that this phase reversal must be taken into account when calculating the film thickness required to extinguish or reinforce our beam of blue light. We see from the preceding discussion that the reflected beam will be extinguished at zero thickness. To get reinforcement, we must adjust the film thickness to get an additional retardation of one-half wave length. (Phase reversal at the rear surface, plus an additional half-wave retardation within the film, will put the two beams in phase again so that crests and troughs coincide.)

REINFORCEMENT AND EXTINCTION

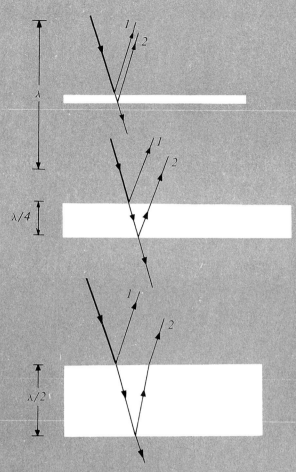

Although there is negligible path difference between beam No. 1 reflected from the top of a very thin film and beam No. 2 reflected from the bottom, the two reflected beams cancel.

Light reflected from the top and bottom of a film that is λ/4 thick. Because of the extra path length λ/2 in beam No. 2, and because the waves in beam No. 1 are turned upside down on reflection, the two reflected rays reinforce.

The two reflected rays when the film is half a wave length thick. The path difference is λ; and beam No. 1 is inverted in reflection. They cancel.

COLOR CHANGES
WITH THE ANGLE OF INCIDENCE

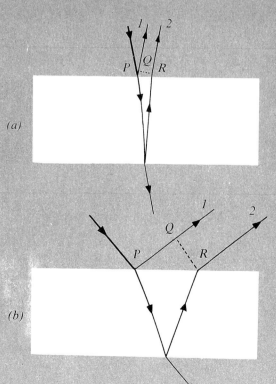

In changing angle from normal incidence, represented approximately by (a), the path of beam 2 from P through the film and back to R is slightly increased, but the path of beam 1 from P to Q is greatly increased. The path difference between 1 and 2 therefore decreases with increasing angle.

Extinction and reinforcement can occur at all thicknesses which create a phase difference of one-half wave length multiplied respectively by any odd or any even number. Extinction, for example, will occur when the phase of the retarded beam differs by 1/2, 3/2, 5/2, etc., wave lengths; reinforcement will occur when they differ by 2/2, 4/2, 6/2, etc., wave lengths.

To translate these retardations into actual film thickness, we must remember first the phase reversal at the rear surface of the film, and second, that the beam reflected from the back surface passes twice through the film. Extinction will, therefore, occur when the optical thickness of the film is 0, 1/2, 1, 3/2, wave lengths and reinforcement when its thickness is 1/4, 3/4, 5/4, etc., wave lengths. The optical thickness, by the way, is the geometrical thickness multiplied by the refractive index.

These dimensions are unbelievably small. A while ago, we defined a micron as one one-thousandth of a millimeter. The wave length of blue light is about 0.45 micron, hence the smallest optical film thickness which reinforces the incoming beam is just over one-tenth of a micron or four millionths of an inch. Since the soap film is mostly water of refractive index 1.33, the smallest linear thickness of the film causing reinforcement will be 0.08 micron. A stack of 300,000 such films would be about an inch high.

Methods have been developed for producing solid transparent films of uniform thickness from substances varying widely in refractive index. Hence, it is possible to produce any desired reflected color—red, for example, by laying down a film whose optical thickness is one-quarter, three-quarters, five-quarters, etc., of 0.6 micron, the wave length of red light. Several such films piled one on top of the other will give not only higher reflectance, but a red of higher purity, less contaminated by other colors.

One final point, and we are through with optical theory. As we have seen, the essential specifications for reinforcement by interference is that the optical paths of the two reflected beams shall differ by precisely the amount which causes wave crests and troughs to coincide. For a film of a given thickness, this path difference varies with the angle of incidence of the incoming beam of light. The path difference is greatest when the beam falls perpendicularly on the film surface. As the angle of incidence increases, the path difference decreases correspondingly. If, for example, we have prepared a film that is red when viewed perpendicularly, its color will shift toward shorter wave lengths; that is, the color will pass through orange, yellow and green as the angle of incidence increases.

This shift in color toward shorter wave lengths with increasing angle of incidence is characteristic only of interference colors. A colored surface which becomes bluer as it is tilted away from the light source is, with certainty, demonstrating interference effects from thin films.

Having now finished, happily for author and reader alike, this dissertation on classical optics, we return to the colors of birds and particularly of hummingbirds. Here Nature has used nearly all her tricks.

Pigmentary colors in birds appear to be limited to yellows, reds, grays and browns. The red of cardinal or tanager is due to its pigmented feathers, as are the yellow of canary and goldfinch, the brown of the sparrow, the gray of titmouse or nuthatch.

Blues are produced by the selective scattering of light from minute particles dispersed into the material of which the feather is made. The mechanism is generally similar to that which produces the blue of the sky. Bluebird, blue jay and indigo bunting are examples in which this type of feather coloring predominates.

Greens are a combination of yellow pigment and blue produced by selective scattering. We find this color in parrots and in many other tropical birds.

Iridescence in the coloration of birds is not at all uncommon. We see iridescent patches in such birds as pigeons, ducks, and grackles, and

(*Text continued on page 103*)

HUMMINGBIRDS

A
PORTFOLIO
OF PHOTOGRAPHS
BY
CRAWFORD H. GREENEWALT

All photographs reproduced life size

THE PLATES

Plates are in geographical order from north to south.

1   *Archilochus colubris* ♂

2   *Archilochus colubris* ♀

3   *Selasphorus platycercus* ♂

4   *Selasphorus rufus* ♂

5   *Stellula calliope* ♂

6   *Archilochus alexandri* ♂

7   *Archilochus alexandri* ♀

8   *Calypte anna* ♀

9   *Archilochus alexandri* ♂

10   *Calypte costae* ♂

11   *Lampornis clemenciae* ♂

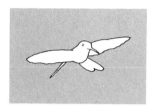

12   *Cynanthus latirostris* ♂

13   *Eugenes fulgens* ♂

14   *Trochilus polytmus* ♂

15   *Michrochera albo-coronata* ♂

16   *Amazilia tzacatl* ♀

17   *Amazilia tobaci* ♂

18   *Topaza pella* ♂

19   *Topaza pella* ♀

20   *Oxypogon guerinii* ♂

21   *Aglaiocercus kingi* ♂

22   *Aglaiocercus kingi* ♀

23   *Campylopterus falcatus* ♂

24   *Campylopterus falcatus* ♀

25   *Phaethornis augusti* ♀

26   *Aglaeactis cupripennis* ♂

27   *Coeligena torquata* ♂

28   *Phaethornis yaruqui*

29   *Lesbia victoriae* ♀

30   *Coeligena wilsoni* ♂

31   *Ensifera ensifera* ♂

32   *Schistes geoffroyi* ♂

33   *Oreotrochilus chimborazo* ♂

 **34** *Eutoxeres aquila*

 **40** *Patagona gigas*

 **46** *Hylocharis sapphirina* ♂

 **35** *Boissonneaua jardini* ♂

 **41** *Campylopterus largipennis*

 **47** *Amazilia versicolor*

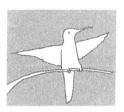 **36** *Eriocnemis luciani* ♂

 **42** *Chrysolampis mosquitus* ♂

 **48** *Chlorostilbon aureo-ventris* ♂

 **37** *Aglaiocercus kingi* ♂

 **43** *Chrysolampis mosquitus* ♀

 **49** *Chlorostilbon aureo-ventris* ♀

 **38** *Ramphomicron microrhynchum* ♂

 **44** *Phaethornis pretrei* ♀

 **50** *Glaucis hirsuta*

 **39** *Ocreatus underwoodii* ♂

 **45** *Anthracothorax nigricollis* ♂

 **51** *Phaethornis ruber* ♂

52 *Lophornis magnifica* ♂

53 *Phaethornis hispidus*

54 *Lophornis magnifica* ♀

55 *Colibri serrirostris* ♂

56 *Popelairia langsdorffi* ♂

57 *Clytolaema rubricauda* ♂

58 *Melanotrochilus fuscus*

59 *Thalurania glaucopis* ♂

60 *Discosura longicauda* ♂

61 *Heliothryx aurita* ♂

62 *Augastes scutatus* ♂

63 *Hylocharis chrysura* ♂

64 *Heliomaster furcifer* ♂

65 *Heliactin cornuta* ♂

66 *Calliphlox amethystina* ♂

67 *Stephanoxis lalandi* ♂

Nomenclature and ranges follow "Check List of Birds of the World"
by James Lee Peters, Harvard University Press, 1945. Vol. V.

♂ *(Mars) is the ornithological symbol for the male.*
♀ *(Venus) denotes the female. Where no symbol is given, gender is not known.*

1   ARCHILOCHUS COLUBRIS ♂
GREENVILLE, NORTHERN DELAWARE

RANGE: Eastern and central North America from southern Alberta and Nova Scotia to Texas and Florida. Winters in southern Florida, southern Mexico and Central America.

As will be seen from its range, the "ruby throat" is the North American hummingbird found east of the Mississippi—and is the only one. It was he who started me off on this project and whether I should bow or blush I find it hard to say.

Ruby throats visit the feeders in our garden in reasonable numbers, but for some reason females predominate and are sufficiently aggressive to give the poor male little chance to take his meal in peace. The corollary is that the unfortunate photographer has females in abundance but only the odd chance for a portrait of the gentleman.

2   ARCHILOCHUS COLUBRIS ♀
GREENVILLE, NORTHERN DELAWARE

RANGE: Same as 1.

This little female ruby throat is caught here at one of her favorite flowers. The wings are at the end of the back stroke and the tail has completed a forward scoop to assist a quick reverse movement. Scientific name for the hummingbird family, *Trochilidae*, is derived from the Greek *trochilus*, which was the name of a bird. *What* bird, we do not know, but its principal distinction, as reported by Herodotus, was picking leeches out of the throats of crocodiles. An odd choice of occupation.

1

2

3

4

3   SELASPHORUS PLATYCERCUS ♂
VICINITY OF DENVER, COLORADO

RANGE: Breeds in mountains of North America from northern Utah and Wyoming south to Mexico and Guatemala, west to California. Winters in west-central Mexico.

This is the hummingbird (its common name is "broad tail") whose wings whistle as he flies. He does not have to be seen to be recognized; the high pitched note is a clear indication of his presence. The whistle, unique among hummingbirds, is due to a narrowing of the tip of the first primary which leaves a small open slot between two adjacent feathers. This slot moving at high speed through the air as the wings beat gives rise to the whistle. A careful look at the wing tip will show this feature.

4   SELASPHORUS RUFUS ♂
COLORADO SPRINGS, COLORADO

RANGE: Southeastern Alaska and southwestern Alberta, south to central California and southwestern Montana. Winters chiefly in west-central Mexico.

This bird was photographed in July on his leisurely way south for the winter. The *rufus* are very aggressive and once they decide to exercise proprietorship no other bird is allowed even to approach the feeding territory.

Selasphorus rufus translates to the "rufous flame bearer," a sufficiently apt description, for he is one of the few hummingbirds with predominantly red-brown body plumage. The "rufous" almost certainly holds the long distance record for the few migratory hummingbirds, completing each year a round trip from southeastern Alaska to Mexico.

5

6

5 STELLULA CALLIOPE ♂
CAMP ANGELUS, NEAR REDLANDS, CALIFORNIA

RANGE: *Breeds in mountains of western North America from southern British Columbia and southwestern Alberta, south to northern Baja California, Arizona and New Mexico. Winters chiefly in south-central Mexico.*

The "calliope" was for me among the most elusive, and not at all because he is the smallest of the North American hummingbirds. I made three trips to California before he consented to pose prettily. The first attempt was frustrated because a sudden snow storm the day of our arrival had caused the *calliope* to depart for a more salubrious climate (the annas stayed, and gave me the unique opportunity to photograph hummingbirds while snow was falling). My second disappointment came when I found that the birds had just left on their migratory journey to the south. The third trip, in June this time, was successful. *Stellula* means "little star," apt enough, I think, but *calliope* means "pleasant voiced," a gross overstatement.

6 ARCHILOCHUS ALEXANDRI ♂
MODJESKA CANYON, NEAR ORANGE, CALIFORNIA

RANGE: *Western North America from British Columbia and Montana to northern Mexico. Winters in Mexico.*

Alexandri, whose common name is "black chin," is a close relative of the ruby throat of the east. *Archilochus* translates to "chief of the regiment." I am told, however, that there was once a famous Greek poet of that name. The poet Archilochus loved a fair lady, as most poets do, but the marriage was forbidden by the prospective bride's father. Archilochus then wrote such eloquently bitter verses that the father, in despair, committed suicide. The *Archilochus* pictured here, happily, seems to have no such problems. A minor photographic triumph is the fact that the iridescent purple collar below the black gorget shows well, a feature hard to see and harder to photograph.

7

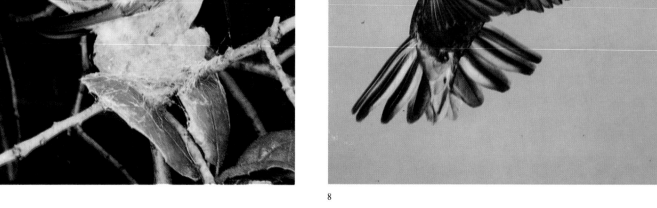

8

7 ARCHILOCHUS ALEXANDRI ♀
MODJESKA CANYON, NEAR ORANGE, CALIFORNIA

RANGE: Same as 6.

We found this lady building her nest at the side of the drive leading to our cottage in the canyon. The nest is about half finished and a careful look will show the spider webbing in her beak, always used by the birds for reinforcing their nests. This is the bird that paid attention neither to the equipment nor the charm of the photographer.

8 CALYPTE ANNA ♂
CAMP ANGELUS NEAR REDLANDS, CALIFORNIA

RANGE: California.

Anna's hummingbird is a pure Californian, wedded to the state north and south, at high altitudes and low. *Anna* is the subject of Dr. Pearson's metabolic experiments at the University of California at Berkeley, which showed that a hummingbird leading its normal life will consume half its weight of sugar daily, an extraordinary intake of fuel.

9

9 ARCHILOCHUS ALEXANDRI ♂
(With Calypte Anna ♀)
MODJESKA CANYON NEAR ORANGE, CALIFORNIA

Here is real belligerence. The ungentlemanly *Alexandri* seems to have no respect for the opposite sex and is moving into the attack with beak and claws extended. The lady, alarmed, is about to make a quick departure. One of the mysteries of hummingbird life is the fact that in one group the males will rule the roost while in another of identical sort the females seem to be in full charge.

10

10 CALYPTE COSTAE ♂
PALM SPRINGS, CALIFORNIA

RANGE: Southwestern United States and lower California. Winters in northwestern Mexico.

Costa's hummingbird is a close cousin of *Calypte anna*, differing principally in the color of the gorget (is purple or red your favorite color?). Costa favors the desert country and feeds from sage and cactus blooms; he seems to avoid the more formal gardens and lush flowers favored by his sibling.

11 LAMPORNIS CLEMENCIAE ♂
RAMSEY CANYON, ARIZONA

RANGE: Mountain slopes from southern Texas and Arizona to southern Mexico.

Tom and Joy St. John were kind enough to put me up for the night at their delightful "Mile High Ranch" in Ramsey Canyon. Stepping carefully and quietly to avoid disturbing my hosts, I arose shortly before dawn and was ready to photograph just as daylight was breaking. This "blue throat" was the first visitor and provided the first picture of the day. The bird seemed active as usual, but the photographer was chilled to the bone and aching for a cup of hot coffee. The photograph as it turned out was, I think, worth all the agony.

12 CYNANTHUS LATIROSTRIS ♂
RAMSEY CANYON, ARIZONA

RANGE: Mountains of Mexico, southern Arizona and southern New Mexico.

As one sees from its range, the "broad bill" barely makes the grade as a United States citizen. It seemed to me that, because of the broad red bill, *Cynanthus* should really be classified with *Hylocharis*. Hartert, however, says of *Cynanthus* (which he called *Phaeoptila*) "Schnabel weich und lebhaft rot oder fleischfarben gefärbt" and of *Hylocharis* "Schnabel an der Basis weich und rot, bei der Nasenlöchern sehr breit." I gave it up.

11

12

16

17

16　AMAZILIA TZACATL ♀
GAMBOA, CANAL ZONE

RANGE: Mexico, south to Venezuela and Ecuador.

This lady built her nest practically on the bank of the Panama Canal. I enjoyed the ships passing by but she, I'm afraid, was too annoyed at camera and lights to pay attention to anything but the photographer. The male and female are alike, both with a characteristic green iridescence on chest and gorget. The young also develop a touch of iridescence before it is time to leave the nest.

17　AMAZILIA TOBACI ♂
CARACAS, VENEZUELA

RANGE: Venezuela; also islands of Trinidad and Tobago.

This variety is the most frequent visitor to the feeders in the garden of Mr. William Phelps, Jr. in Caracas. An extremely

bellicose and irascible citizen, *Amazilia* would rout any other hummingbird who so much as approached the premises.

18　TOPAZA PELLA ♂
ALTO RIO CUYUNI, VENEZUELA

RANGE: British Guiana, Surinam and southern Venezuela.

In many ways this is the most gorgeous of the hummingbirds, fully justifying its name, "the beautiful topaz." The topaz are seen rarely, usually spending their time in the flowered canopy of tall trees 100–150 feet from the ground. This one was netted flying close to the surface of a stream while on his way to bathe. He proved a more recalcitrant subject than most and was brought to the perch in front of the camera only by coaxing him onto a small stick, which was lowered gently until the feeder caught his eye. Fortunately the sugar solution offered sufficient promise for him to negotiate the remaining foot or so under his own auspices.

18

19

20

19   TOPAZA PELLA ♀
ALTO RIO CUYUNI, VENEZUELA

RANGE: Same as 18.

This is the mate of the gorgeous creature shown just previously. In beauty she surpasses many males of other species. Before the camera, in marked contrast to her lord and master, she turned out to be rather a ham; once she saw what I was about she perched near the feeder and would fly down to be photographed at embarrassingly frequent intervals. I finally had to shoo her off so that the other birds would have opportunity to occupy the limelight in the center of the stage.

20   OXYPOGON GUERINII ♂
PICO DE AQUILA, MERIDA, VENEZUELA (ALT. 13,000 FT.)

RANGE: Paramo zone of the Andes of Colombia and Venezuela.

Oxypogon is one of the most unusual hummingbirds. The combination of crest and beard reminds one of an Oriental sage. It is a resident of the high valleys in the Andes—only *Oreotrochilus* is found at higher altitudes. This bird was brought from its home territory to Caracas, a difference in elevation of about 9,000 feet. The night after I had photographed him he died, perhaps because of the change in altitude. The females appear to be more hardy. Three of them, subjected to the same transplanting, were perky and happy, if husbandless, after three full weeks in captivity.

21   AGLAIOCERCUS KINGI ♂
MOUNTAINS NEAR CARACAS, VENEZUELA

RANGE: Mountainous areas from Venezuela to Bolivia.

It is remarkable to note how this elegant bird manages his long tail while flying through the underbrush. One would expect it to be broken or at least crumpled after a few excursions. To the contrary, he has the ability to maneuver so that it retains its pristine beauty even for the year which elapses between molts.

This is another case which demonstrates the impossibility of showing all features in a single photograph. *Kingi* has a flashing purple gorget and a brilliant green crown. A choice had to be made and while other birds have brightly illuminated gorgets, few indeed have *kingi's* caudal elegance.

22

22   AGLAIOCERCUS KINGI ♀
MOUNTAINS NEAR CARACAS, VENEZUELA

RANGE: Same as 21.

Here is another example of a lady far less flashy than her consort but dainty and attractive for all that. There appear to be at least five and perhaps six races of *A. kingi*. The males vary in length of tail and color of its iridescence. The ladies differ so little that one could not distinguish between them in the field. I might, without fear of contradiction, call this one *berlepschi, kingi, margarethae, mocoa* or *smaragdinus*. I'll choose *margarethae*, first because it is quite probably correct, and second because of the fact that each of two very important Greenewalt ♀'s, my wife and a newly arrived granddaughter, have the name Margaretta.

23   CAMPYLOPTERUS FALCATUS ♂
CARACAS, VENEZUELA

RANGE: Lower slopes of the Andes in Venezuela, Colombia and Ecuador.

The *Campylopteri* are sometimes called "sabre wings."

The wings at rest are bent, but apparently the bend straightens out in flight. *Falcatus* has really been through the nomenclatural mill, showing, I suppose, that taxonomists will, like the ladies, change their minds. He has been called successively *Trochilus lazulus, Campylopterus lazulus, Trochilus falcatus, Ornismya falcata, Trochilus castanurus, Trochilus ceciliae, Campylopterus falcipennis, Saepiopterus goeringi,* and now, and I hope with finality, *Campylopterus falcatus.*

24   CAMPYLOPTERUS FALCATUS ♀
CARACAS, VENEZUELA

RANGE: Same as 23.

The female of the species, while not as brightly colored as the male, is sufficiently elegant. This bird and her mate were photographed in the garden of Mr. William Phelps, Jr. in Caracas, where Mr. Phelps was kind enough to provide sugar solution for the birds and an occasional gin and tonic for the photographer. Rarely has an expedition enjoyed such charming facilities for investigation.

23

24

25 PHAETHORNIS AUGUSTI ♀

NEAR CARACAS, VENEZUELA

RANGE: Mountains of northern South America.

    Phaethornis is another genus with many species. For the most part they keep to the woods and so are hard to see. The bird is probably a female since we found a nest under construction nearby, attached to the corrugated roof of a pump house which providentially was provided with a grilled door.

26 AGLAEACTIS CUPRIPENNIS ♂
PAPALLACTA, ECUADOR

RANGE: The temperate zone of the Andes (seven to twelve thousand feet) from Colombia to Peru.

This resident of the highlands is unique in two respects. It is one of the few hummingbirds to show iridescence on its back, and the iridescence is seen only when illumination and observer are reversed from their normal positions. It has also an extraordinary wing spread and a correspondingly low wing beat rate. Finally, the red-brown body plumage, also unusual among hummingbirds.

27   COELIGENA TORQUATA ♂
CERRO PAUMA, ECUADOR

RANGE: Lower slopes of the Andes, Venezuela to Peru.

An elegant creature which the native collectors in Ecuador call "corbata blanca" or "white cravat." It seems to me this understates the case; *torquata's* characteristics are more spectacular than even the dressiest of "white tie" occasions suggest. Peters recognizes five races, all very similar except the one from Bolivia for which the band extending around the upper breast area is rufous.

28

28   PHAETHORNIS YARUQUI
SANTO DOMINGO DE LOS COLORADOS, ECUADOR

RANGE: Tropical western Colombia and Ecuador.

Perhaps I have gone a little heavily on the genus *Phae-thornis* in this collection, but I could not resist *yaruqui's* extraordinary posture and flashy air. There are two races—*P. yaruqui yaruqui* and *P. yaruqui sancti-johannis*. Much as I would have liked to include a St. John in my collection, I fear that this one is almost certainly *yaruqui*.

29

29 LESBIA VICTORIAE ♀
QUITO, ECUADOR

RANGE: Dry Andean areas in Colombia, Ecuador, Peru.

This motherly creature is an Ecuadorian bird; in the Peruvian races the tail is an inch or two shorter. The nest was sixteen feet up in an araucaria tree in the garden of our hotel at Quito. We despaired of reaching it until some bright soul talked the local airline into lending us the platform used for servicing the nose of a DC-3. A bit of adventurous trucking, a chain gang to hand up photographic gear and there we were.

30

30 COELIGENA WILSONI ♂
GUALEA, ECUADOR

RANGE: Lower Andean slopes, Colombia and Ecuador.

   A bath in a waterfall. The bird seemed to delight in this version of a shower bath, as do many other species. After being cooped up for a day or two in the cage used for photography, the birds released into the large outdoor aviary made a beeline for the water as if eager to wash away care.

31 ENSIFERA ENSIFERA ♂
NEAR PAPALLACTA, ECUADOR

RANGE: Andes of Venezuela, Colombia, Ecuador and Peru; northern Bolivia.

    This is a bird I shall never forget. The bill of course is the feature. No other hummingbird has one even approaching its length; I doubt, in fact, that there is *any* bird for which bill and body are so disproportionate. The present photograph came easily enough but I wanted very badly to photograph a female of this remarkable genus feeding her young. Reports of an occupied nest at Papallacta sent me off in high hopes to that village, which is at an elevation of 11,000 feet. After making our weary way an additional 1500 feet up a slope with a 45 degree grade, we came to the nest in an Indian hut, only to find it abandoned by the inconsiderate parent. My physical exhaustion was equalled only by my spiritual disappointment.

32

32 SCHISTES GEOFFROYI ♂
GUALEA, ECUADOR

RANGE: Lower Andean slopes, Venezuela to Bolivia.

    We have here the songster referred to in Chapter One. This is the Ecuador race; in the other two the throat is never white. To my eye, it seems closely related to *Augastes scutatus*, particularly because of the green face mask common to both. Peters, whom I am bound to respect, disagrees.

33

33 OREOTROCHILUS CHIMBORAZO ♂
MT. CHIMBORAZO, ECUADOR

RANGE: Upper border of Paramo zone, Ecuador.

  Oreotrochilus holds the altitude record for the hummingbird family. It is found only on the high Andean meadows
(called the Paramos) at elevations of 14,000 feet or more right
up to the equatorial snow line. *Oreotrochilus* mitigates the
rigors of cold nights by clinging to the rocky walls of caves in
the mountains. There are three races—*jamesoni, soderstromi*
and *chimborazo*. This one is without doubt *chimborazo* because of the narrow green collar at the base of its purple
gorget. He was conveyed from his high-level habitat (involun-
tarily, of course) to the relative comfort of Quito at 10,000
feet. I had hoped also to photograph an occupied nest even
though that meant braving the really high altitudes. Unfortunately or perhaps fortunately for my breathing apparatus no
nests, occupied or otherwise, could be located readily.

34

34 EUTOXERES AQUILA
SANTO DOMINGO DE LOS COLORADOS, ECUADOR

RANGE: Costa Rica, Panama, Colombia, Ecuador.

This is the famous sickle bill. Aside from its one characteristic feature, it is completely unspectacular. I saw it in its native habitat feeding on "platanillos," a plant of the banana family with a long raceme of flowers which the bird climbs as if up a ladder, feasting upon one bloom after another.

35

36

37

35 BOISSONNEAUA JARDINI ♂
NANEGAL, ECUADOR

RANGE: Lower Andean slopes, Colombia and Ecuador.

Some consider *Boissonneaua* rather than *Topaza* (Plate 18) the most spectacular of hummingbirds. A hundred years ago John Gould described his frustration in depicting this species: "I must confess that the means at my command are utterly inadequate to do justice to the crown, back, shoulders, and chest sides, clothed with hues of metallic blue and green of such resplendent brilliancy that it is quite impossible to represent them on paper." I think I can add that neither the passage of a century nor the invention of color photography make the task easier. To me all hummingbirds have charm and good looks. Selection of a Miss (or Mr.) Universe among them would be a chore in which I should find little relish.

36 ERIOCNEMIS LUCIANI ♂
PICHINCHA, ECUADOR

RANGE: Andes of Ecuador and Peru.

Note the powder puff covering on the legs, a characteristic of the genus. In temperament it was as bold as any bird I have seen, and would come into the feeder to take his snack, driving off any other bird, regardless of size, intruding upon his privacy.

37 AGLAIOCERCUS KINGI ♂
PAPALLACTA, ECUADOR

RANGE: Mountainous areas from Venezuela to Bolivia.

The characteristic feature of this genus is the beautiful iridescent tail. Otherwise the bird is dull with a tiny iridescent patch on its throat. Perhaps this is another example of nature's frugal habit of bestowing only one adornment at a time. Peters recognizes five races of this species. Fortunately the one shown here has a shorter and broader tail than the others, making it reasonably safe to identify this as *Aglaiocercus kingi mocoa.*

38

39

38 RAMPHOMICRON MICRORHYNCHUM ♂
PAPALLACTA, ECUADOR

RANGE: The Andes from Venezuela to Peru.

Why it is necessary to call this bird a "small bill-small bill" I can't imagine. It does indeed have the smallest bill of any hummingbird, and perhaps the naturalist who originally named it wanted to draw particular attention to that fact. *Ramphomicron* has a beautiful yellow-green gorget and I was torn between pictures taken from in front and behind. Many species, however, boast beautiful gorgets, but few can show a back as lovely as this.

39 OCREATUS UNDERWOODII ♂
GUALEA, ECUADOR

RANGE: Lower Andean slopes, Venezuela to Bolivia.

Ocreatus exemplifies the problem of classification for hummingbirds. Hartert, in his listing made in 1900, recognizes five distinct species of *Ocreatus*. Peters, thirty years later, says that there is but one species which he subdivides

into six races. According to Hartert this one would clearly be *Ocreatus melanantherus* because of its habitat and the white powder puffs on its legs. Peters insists that we say *Ocreatus underwoodii melanantherus*.

Whatever its proper name this is one of the most delightful of the racket tails. To its blue flags there is added a downy leg covering and an iridescent green gorget. No doubt its prospective mates find these fine romantic attractions irresistible.

40 PATAGONA GIGAS
CUZCO, PERU

RANGE: The Andes, Ecuador to Chile and Argentina.

The largest or "giant" hummingbird. A *Patagona* was a regular visitor to the garden of our hotel in Quito. After much effort we managed to capture it only to see it dart away when some injudicious soul opened the door of the cage in which we were photographing. This bird, captured a year later in Peru, tempered our disappointment at the loss.

41

41 CAMPYLOPTERUS LARGIPENNIS
BELEM DO PARA, BRAZIL

RANGE: Tropical South America from Venezuela and the Guianas to Brazil and eastern Bolivia.

The race shown here is probably *Campylopterus largipennis obscurus. Obscurus* obviously means what it says as far as coloring is concerned. In spite of all that, the bird is spectacular enough to satisfy the most demanding and aesthetic of observers.

42 CHRYSOLAMPIS MOSQUITUS ♂
SANTA TERESA, ESPIRITO SANTO, BRAZIL

RANGE: Tropical and eastern South America.

By all rights *Chrysolampis mosquitus* should have been extinct a generation ago. At the turn of this century, thousands of skins were sent annually to the markets of London and Paris for their decorative value in ladies' millinery. Other uses were in making artificial flowers and "costume" jewelry.

43 CHRYSOLAMPIS MOSQUITUS ♀
CACERES, MATO GROSSO, BRAZIL

RANGE: Same as 42.

Certainly not as flashy as her consort but none the less dainty and elegant, this lady nested successfully in Dr. Ruschi's aviary. The elegant male (Plate 42), bearing no resemblance, is her son.

42

43

45

44　PHAETHORNIS PRETREI ♀
ESPIRITO SANTO, BRAZIL

RANGE: Brazil south of Amazonia; eastern Bolivia.

Dr. Ruschi found this nest by spotting the bird as it flew out when his car rattled over a small wooden bridge. There was barely enough room under the bridge for photographer and apparatus. The day was hot and I remember with much pleasure dangling bare feet in the little stream while waiting for the mother to come back to tend her eggs. The excrescence to the right is not characteristic but represents a false start and the privilege accorded the female, bird or human, of changing her mind.

45　ANTHRACOTHORAX NIGRICOLLIS ♂
SANTA TERESA, ESPIRITO SANTO, BRAZIL

RANGE: Panama and tropical South America generally.

One of the few hummingbirds with extensive black plumage. The photographer all too often faces a real dilemma in selection—the picture that shows off one feature well may be weak in other respects. In this study the bill is difficult to see and I should perhaps have chosen another, but I couldn't resist the beautiful tail and the outspread wings.

46

47

48

49

46 HYLOCHARIS SAPPHIRINA ♂
ESPIRITO SANTO, BRAZIL

RANGE: Tropical South America, east of the Andes.

Sapphire, of course, refers to the blue gorget, but it seems to me that its other adornments are quite as spectacular as its poetic name suggests. The trademark of this genus is the broad red bill.

47 AMAZILIA VERSICOLOR
SANTA TERESA, ESPIRITO SANTO, BRAZIL

RANGE: South America, east of the Andes, ranging from Colombia to Paraguay.

There are a great many species and subspecies in this genus, seventy-nine at latest count, differing relatively little in size or coloring. The pose shows the quick getaway for which hummingbirds are noted—a scoop with the tail and a strong reversal of the wings. Maneuverability is their chief defense.

48 CHLOROSTILBON AUREO-VENTRIS ♂
SANTA TERESA, ESPIRITO SANTO, BRAZIL

RANGE: S. Brazil, Bolivia, Argentina, Uruguay, Paraguay.

This is one of the most gorgeous of the genus *Chlorostilbon*. *Aureo-ventris* means golden belly—here, as in other instances, the name would appear greatly to understate the beauty of the bird.

49 CHLOROSTILBON AUREO-VENTRIS ♀
SANTA TERESA, ESPIRITO SANTO, BRAZIL

RANGE: Same as 48.

One of Dr. Ruschi's most spectacular accomplishments is his ability to spot a tiny nest like this one while driving along the road in his car. This nest is the most beautiful I have ever seen. The female was incubating her eggs and after becoming used to camera and lights had literally to be driven off the nest in order to catch wing action such as this.

50

51

52a   52b

50   GLAUCIS HIRSUTA
SANTA TERESA, ESPIRITO SANTO, BRAZIL

RANGE: Nicaragua and Costa Rica south into Brazil and Bolivia. It is also found on Trinidad, Tobago and Grenada.

    Hirsuta means hairy, and why this designation should be appropriate, I can't imagine. I would certainly not claim that the bird is shown to full advantage in this picture, but who could resist the peekaboo action of the wings, and the spectacular flower which is affording the bird a light snack.

51   PHAETHORNIS RUBER ♂
ESPIRITO SANTO, BRAZIL

RANGE: Tropical South America, east of the Andes.

    Bird photography, as I have noted, is not unlike *chemin de fer* or door-to-door selling—the odds on success rise with the number of tries. In this regard, one of the pleasant things about species of the genus *Phaethornis* is that less patience is required to get a good picture. The absence of iridescence makes life easier for the photographer. The chances of success here are one in ten rather than one in fifty for the more spectacular varieties. This is the bird which, as described in Chapter 1, hangs out its tongue in a manner "exquisite and ridiculous."

52   LOPHORNIS MAGNIFICA ♂
SANTA TERESA, ESPIRITO SANTO, BRAZIL

RANGE: Central and southern Brazil.

    The birds of this genus are called "coquettes." The red crest (not iridescent) and tail are characteristic of all species, though the collar ornaments vary greatly from one to another. This one, as well as most of the others, can extend the long feathers straight out from the neck to produce a lovely white fan tipped with a delicate iridescent green.

53

53 PHAETHORNIS HISPIDUS
TAPIRAPOAN, MATO GROSSO, BRAZIL

RANGE: Tropics and eastern base of the Andes from Venezuela to Bolivia.

One of the few hummingbirds with gray plumage. I looked up "hispidus" in a Latin dictionary and found that it meant "rough, straggly, hairy, bristly or prickly." None of these characteristics seems particularly apt. I discovered also that there is an English word—hispid—which Webster defines as "rough with bristles, stiff hairs or minute spines." Not much help there either, so I'll let it go at that.

54   LOPHORNIS MAGNIFICA ♀
(With P. Hispidus, see Plate 53)
TAPIRAPOAN, MATO GROSSO, BRAZIL

RANGE: Tropics and eastern base of the Andes from Venezuela to Bolivia.

Females of this genus seem to have extraordinarily short tempers, even under tender circumstances. I was once fortunate enough to observe the courtship of *Lophornis magnifica* and to see the male in all his nuptial glory. Whenever he flew within range, the female, I regret to say, launched a determined peck at him. The *hispidus* in this picture has no wish to fight but only a fair turn at the feeder.

55

56

57

55   COLIBRI SERRIROSTRIS ♂
SANTA TERESA, ESPIRITO SANTO, BRAZIL

RANGE: Southern Brazil, northern Argentina, Bolivia.

The members of this genus all have iridescent ear coverts which, when excited, they extend almost vertically from the side of the head. There is one closely related species, *Colibri coruscans*, with a special distinction: It is the only one among all hummingbirds in which the male is said to cooperate in the care of the young. This seems hard to believe, in view of the carefree nature of other males, but two reliable ornithologists testify to having seen it at first hand, and must be credited.

56   POPELAIRIA LANGSDORFFI ♀
SANTA TERESA, ESPIRITO SANTO, BRAZIL

RANGE: Eastern Ecuador, eastern Peru and Brazil.

The characteristic feature of the genus *Popelairia* is the needle-like tail; some naturalists, in fact, have called them "thorn tails." It was most amusing to see this one flying about with tail held high as if it were about to squat. *Langsdorffi* as his special feature has an iridescent red band which, as shown, runs midway down his belly.

57   CLYTOLAEMA RUBRICAUDA ♂
SANTA TERESA, ESPIRITO SANTO, BRAZIL

RANGE: Southeastern Brazil.

This elegant bird is a frequent visitor to the outdoor feeders at Dr. Ruschi's house. The female lacks the iridescent patches on gorget and crown but her browns and greens are exceedingly beautiful.

58

59

60

58 MELANOTROCHILUS FUSCUS
SANTA TERESA, ESPIRITO SANTO, BRAZIL

RANGE: Eastern Brazil.

This is the most frequent visitor to Dr. Ruschi's feeders in the Brazilian spring. There are no iridescent patches but the bird is sufficiently elegant. A friend gave him the apt name "top hat and tails."

59 THALURANIA GLAUCOPIS ♂
SANTA TERESA, ESPIRITO SANTO, BRAZIL

RANGE: Eastern and southern Brazil, also in Uruguay, Paraguay, Misiones.

There are many species of the genus *Thalurania*, all of them characterized by brilliant areas of green and blue iridescence. Otherwise the variations are small, a long tail for one, small size for another, iridescence extending to the back for a third. *Glaucopis* seems reasonably average for the group.

60 DISCOSURA LONGICAUDA ♂
CONCEIÇÃO DA BARRA, ESPIRITO SANTO, BRAZIL

RANGE: Venezuela, the Guianas and eastern Brazil.

Another racket tail which in beauty competes quite successfully with *Ocreatus underwoodii* (Plate 39). No puff legs here but *Discosura* has pleasant vari-colored feathering on the abdomen and iridescence embracing the head, neck and gorget.

61 HELIOTHRYX AURITA ♂
SANTA TERESA, ESPIRITO SANTO, BRAZIL

RANGE: Most of tropical South America.

Though other hummingbirds may be more brilliantly colored, this to my eye is one of the most spectacular. Unfortunately, the tail here is a trifle ragged, a not uncommon misfortune either in the wild or in captivity. *Aurita* seems more insectivorous than other species; this specimen would chase any small bug on sight while its neighbors perched and watched the action contentedly.

61

66

67

66 CALLIPHLOX AMETHYSTINA ♂
TERESOPOLIS NEAR RIO DE JANEIRO, BRAZIL

RANGE: Tropical South America, east of the Andes.

One of the smallest hummingbirds, probably weighing less than a dime. Its wing beat is the fastest I have recorded—eighty per second. The female is somewhat larger and has a wing rate of sixty per second. The buzz of the wings in flight is sufficiently high and distinctive to permit recognition by listeners before anything is in sight.

67 STEPHANOXIS LALANDI ♂
ITATIAIA, NEAR RIO DE JANEIRO, BRAZIL

RANGE: Southern Brazil, northern Argentina, adjoining areas of Paraguay.

I saw Dr. Ruschi catch this bird in a beautiful mountain area back of Rio. He used a fly casting rod tipped with an adhesive. Bird in hand, he gave it a rewarding draft of sugar solution, wrapped it in a miniature night shirt to quiet its wings, and tucked it in his pocket. The bird was indignant but none the worse for wear. Peters recognizes two races of this species, *lalandi* and *loddiggesi*. By virtue of its green crest, this is *Stephanoxis lalandi lalandi*. On *loddiggesi*, the identifying crest is violet.

Trochilus polytmus ♂

These pictures of a male Chrysolampis mosquitus *show how the position of the bird controls the brilliance of the iridescent colors as recorded by the camera.*
[See Chapter 2.]

even in starlings and crows, as well as in more exotic varieties such as the peacocks, the sunbirds and, of course, the hummingbirds. Intensity of the iridescent colors, however, varies over wide limits, from a barely perceptible colored sheen in the throat of a pigeon to the pure spectral brilliance of the hummingbird gorget.

The physical basis for iridescent colors has interested scientists for a hundred or more years, and a listing of the technical papers dealing with the subject would fill many pages. Newton was the first to suggest that iridescent colors in birds and insects might be due to the presence of thin films, whose color-producing properties he had first observed. In his "Treatise on Opticks" (London 1704), Newton states the case as follows:

> ". . . The finely coloured Feathers of some birds, and particularly those of Peacocks Tails, do in the very same part of the Feather appear of several Colours in several positions of the Eye, after the very same manner that thin Plates were found to do . . . and therefore arise from the thinness of the transparent parts of the Feathers; that is, from the slenderness of the very fine Hairs, or *Capillamenta,* which grow out of the sides of the grosser lateral branches or fibres of those Feathers."

Newton believed that light was composed of bundles of discrete particles; this "particle theory" of light made it quite difficult to explain simultaneous refraction and reflection from a surface.

With the development of the wave theory of light (principally by Thomas Young in 1807), and recognition of interference as the extinction or reinforcement of light waves, new light was cast on the problem. It is clear that, if interference is involved, the color of bird or insect must shift toward the blue as the viewing angle is decreased. There is no other color-producing mechanism which behaves in this way. The experimental method is simplicity itself — tilt the feather so that the viewing angle becomes steadily more acute. If the color shifts toward the blue (red becomes orange, orange becomes yellow, yellow shifts to green, etc.), the conclusion is inescapable that some form of thin film interference is involved.

Interference as the cause of iridescent colors in birds was first proposed by Altum in 1857 and, while there have been doubting Thomases in the intervening years, nearly all subsequent investigators confirm his findings. Today, interference as the cause of iridescence is universally accepted.

The nature of the thin film or films was, however, far from clear. It was recognized early in the game that a single thin film could not produce reflectances as brilliant as those observed in hummingbirds. The sophisticated investigators therefore postulated the existence of a number of films stacked on top of each other to account for the brilliance. Until recent years, this theory could not be verified experimentally because interference films are so thin that the best of the optical microscopes could not make them visible to the human eye.

A quite recent study of the colored surface of hummingbird barbules using the highest power of the optical microscope was made by a German investigator. He found that the surface consists of a beautiful mosaic of colored elliptical platelets resembling generally a tiled floor. Even with the best of modern techniques, he was unable to do more than guess at their thickness because of the limitations of optical microscopes. All he could really say was that the platelets were exceedingly thin.

Such was the state of the knowledge when our studies began.

First, we repeated the examination of barbular surfaces with the optical microscope. We confirmed the presence of the platelet mosaic on the iridescent feather surfaces of fifty or so hummingbird species. Only the platelets are colored; the interstices are dark. The platelets are minute, about two and a half microns across the long axis of the ellipse, and about one micron across the short axis. Ten thousand of them laid end to end would measure about an inch.

Their size varies little throughout the hummingbird species which we have examined. The length of two and a half microns is a good average and the limits of variation would be no more than 30 per cent either way.

Along its length, the barbule is divided into cells separated by diagonal lines crossing the width of the barbule. At the points where the barbule joins the ramus and where the pennulum develops, the colored platelets disappear and one sees only a few random uncolored or faintly colored ellipses in these areas.

The barbule proper then has a surface which is 15-20 microns wide and 100 microns long, divided by diagonal boundary lines into a series of cells which look like parallelograms, each cell made up of a mosaic of 100 or more beautifully colored elliptical platelets.

We then turned to a quantitative analysis of the iridescent colors. For this we used a spectrophotometer, an instrument which measures precisely the light intensity at any wave length. We find the curves for the many hummingbird colors to be very much alike. There is a very sharp peak of high reflectance—the reflectance falling off rapidly to nearly zero on either side. By measuring these curves at high and low angles of incidence, we confirmed quantitatively the fact that the color

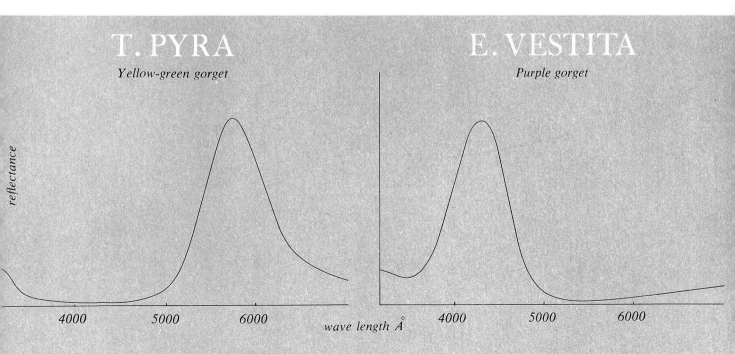

The visible spectrum includes the interval between 4500 and 6500 Angstrom units. (An Angstrom unit is a measure of length; ten thousand of them equal one micron.)

invariably shifts toward the blue as the angle of incidence increases. This proves once more that thin film interference is the color source.

Even more significant results can be obtained from these curves. The shift in peak wave length for a given change in angle of incidence permits measurement of the mean refractive index of the material producing the interference color. We find that the refractive index changes from a higher to a lower value as the color of the feather moves from red to blue. For red feathers, for example, the mean refractive index is about 1.85; for blue feathers, it drops to about 1.5; for green feathers, it has an intermediate value.

These findings lead to the rather unexpected conclusion that Nature either develops a new substance of different refractive index for each color she wishes to produce, or that she makes her interfering films out of two substances, one of high and the other of low refractive index, varying the average by varying the proportion of the two substances. Which alternative is correct will become clear from later experiments.

The spectrophotometer can also tell us one more essential fact, and that is the mean thickness of the film producing the interference colors. As we have seen in the discussion on optics, an interference peak can occur at several different film thicknesses. The requirement

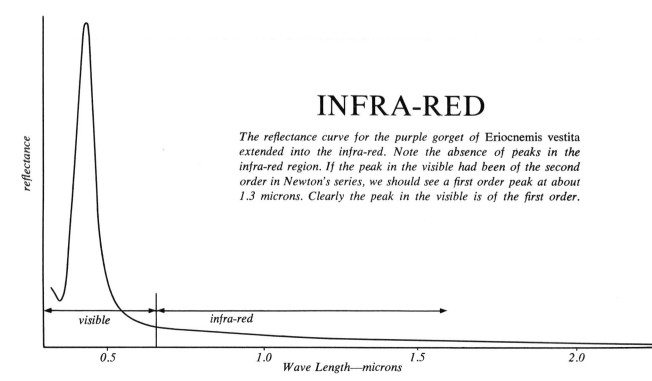

INFRA-RED

The reflectance curve for the purple gorget of Eriocnemis vestita *extended into the infra-red. Note the absence of peaks in the infra-red region. If the peak in the visible had been of the second order in Newton's series, we should see a first order peak at about 1.3 microns. Clearly the peak in the visible is of the first order.*

is merely that the retardation causes the wave crests reflected from front and back surfaces to reinforce each other. We have seen that this can occur for films whose optical thickness is 1/4, 3/4, 5/4, etc., of the peak wave length. To decide where we are in this series, we must determine whether peaks exist at longer or shorter wave lengths than the one we observe in the visible spectrum.

It is experimentally simpler for us to push our curves toward longer wave lengths; that is, into the infra-red region of the spectrum. When we do this, we find no peaks, but reflectances near zero as far out as we can measure. We must conclude, therefore, that the peak we observe is of the first order corresponding to a film whose optical thickness is one-quarter the peak wave length. For a peak in the green, this would imply an optical film thickness of a little more than one-tenth of a micron. We can now easily understand why films of such minute thickness were not observed by previous investigators. Because they are so much thinner than the wave length of visible light, they cannot be seen even with the best of the optical microscopes.

The theory of the reflectance of single or of multiple homogeneous films is well known and it is possible for us to compare theory and observation as far as we have gone. We start with our observed

THEORETICAL CURVES
FOR HOMOGENEOUS FILMS

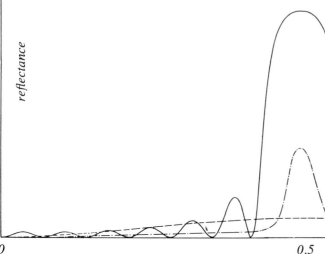

The dashed line shows reflectances for a single homogeneous film, the solid line for a multiple sandwich containing seven films of refractive index 2.0 alternating with seven of refractive index 1.5. The dot-dash line is for the red gorget feather of Calypte anna. *Reflectances are plotted against the ratio optical film thickness to wave length to demonstrate the symmetry which is inherent in the curves.*

reflectance

0   0.5   1.0

curve for a typical hummingbird feather and plot on the same scale a theoretical curve for a single film with optical thickness one-quarter the peak wave length together with the theoretical curve for a number of such films stacked on top of each other. For the theoretical case, we choose a refractive index of 2.0 for the interfering film and 1.5 (the refractive index of the keratin of which feathers are made) for the other component of the multiple sandwich.

When we do this, we see that neither theoretical curve approaches even remotely the experimental curve for the typical feather. The curve for a single film has too broad a peak and the reflectance is far too low. The multiple layers produce too high a reflectance and the shape of the curve is totally different from the one determined experimentally.

Clearly, we must search further.

It seems obvious that we must learn more about the structural details of the platelets comprising the colored surface of the barbule. For this, we turn to the electron microscope. Even if pressed, I doubt very much that I could explain how this instrument works and I would lose a majority of my readers in the attempt. Let us simply say that the electron microscope can resolve detail in objects hundreds of times smaller than can be seen with the optical microscope.

When we apply this instrument to our platelets, we see that they are not homogeneous, but have the appearance more or less of an elliptical pancake made from dough to which baking soda has been liberally added. We find a matrix containing air bubbles which in cross section looks something like a thin section of a foam mattress. This structure is completely consistent with our refractive index measurements made with the spectrophotometer. If we assume a refractive index of say 2.0 for the matrix and 1.0 for the air bubbles, we can easily see how the average refractive index for the platelets can vary from 1.85 to 1.5 as the air content for the platelet increases. The electron microscope also shows us that there are eight to ten layers of platelets at the surface of

HIGH MAGNIFICATION

At the top we see photomicrographs of the reflecting surfaces of two barbules, Clytolaema rubricauda *at the left and* Heliangelus viola *at the right. The latter was taken at the highest magnification possible for optical microscopes. The platelet mosaics are clearly seen.*

At the bottom we show the electron photomicrographs. At the left a tiny portion of a cross section of a barbule magnified 16,000x. Below a cross section through a single platelet magnified 45,000x. At right, a plan view of several platelets magnified 40,000x. The white spaces are air cells, the dark matrix is a substance, probably melanin, of very high refractive index. "Pancake" form is evident.

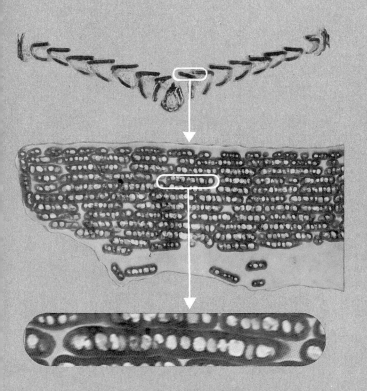

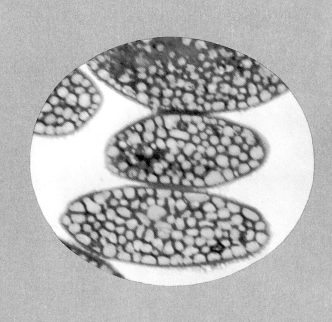

the barbule.

From this we deduce that the platelet has an interference structure which is inhomogeneous, comprising air and some material of much higher refractive index, that the surface of the barbule has eight to ten layers of such platelets, and that the air content increases to produce a lower mean refractive index as the color of the feather passes from red to green to blue.

It remains now to determine whether theory and experiment are consistent. To do this, we must find out whether the theoretical interference curves for layers of platelets which are not homogeneous will match those we have determined experimentally.

Unfortunately, the literature on interference has little to say about inhomogeneous interference structures, possibly because such structures have not been produced artificially and no one had suspected that they would be found in nature.

One of my associates, Dr. Werner Brandt, was sufficiently interested in the problem to develop the theory, which for me would have been quite impossible. The mathematics involved are gruesome in the extreme and solution of the problem required the use of one of the large electronic computers about which we have heard so much in recent years.

To pass quickly and perhaps uncharitably over many hours of work by Dr. Brandt and many millions of computations by the indefatigable computer, we find that theory and experiment are indeed consistent. The observed spectrophotometric curve can be matched very nicely by assuming a stack of about three platelets, each platelet being made of a matrix of refractive index 2.2 and containing an adequate proportion of air bubbles of refractive index 1.0.

It turns out also that each platelet behaves as if it were in reality two films, each with an optical thickness one-quarter of the peak wave length. When we speak of whole platelets, their optical thickness will be one-half the peak wave length, and their true thickness the optical thickness divided by the mean refractive index.

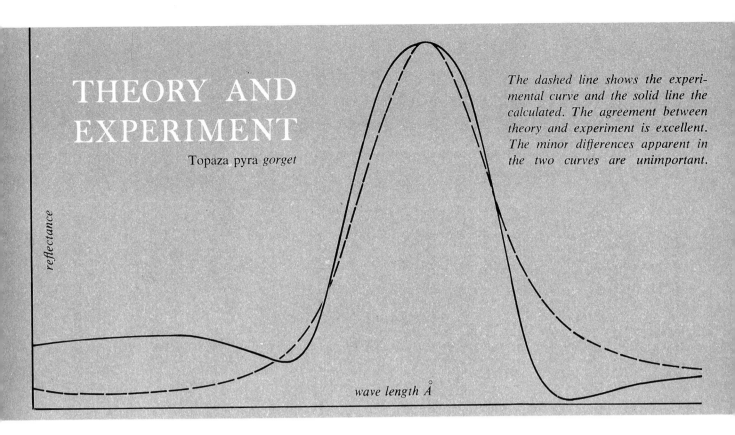

THEORY AND EXPERIMENT

Topaza pyra *gorget*

reflectance

wave length Å

The dashed line shows the experimental curve and the solid line the calculated. The agreement between theory and experiment is excellent. The minor differences apparent in the two curves are unimportant.

A final check is to compare calculated platelet thickness with the dimensions obtained by measuring the electron photomicrographs. Here also theory and experiment agree; the measured platelet thickness, about 0.18 micron, being just about that of Dr. Brandt's theory.

To summarize: Hummingbird iridescence is due to interference colors produced by a stack of about three films, each film consisting of a mosaic of platelets of elliptical form. Each platelet is about two and one-half microns long, one micron wide, with an optical thickness one-half the peak wave length. The platelets are not homogeneous and consist of air bubbles encased in a matrix of refractive index a little greater than two. The different hummingbird colors are produced by changing both the air content of the platelets and their thickness. Of course the range of colors might have been produced at constant thicknesses by varying the air content or vice versa. Nature appears to have elected to vary both factors simultaneously. Whether or not similar structures are found in the feathers of other birds having iridescent colors, we shall have to leave to further investigation.

So, feathers and feather structure; color and interference; our "glittering fragment of the rainbow" quite unromantically shorn of his secrets. I wonder from time to time whether it would have been better to stop with the pictures and leave the scientific exposition to the technical journals. I am left with a faint uneasiness that it might have been wiser to admire than to understand, and to anyone holding this point of view I extend my sympathies.

I must, however, confess to a predilection for exposition as well as appreciation. Perhaps, in retrospect, the two are not wholly incompatible. Is the rainbow, after all, less radiant because we know that it results from the condensation of moisture, or mountains less majestic because we can trace their birth to subterranean growls and heavings? If not, then perhaps the flash of the iridescent gorget will be no less bright because we have subjected it to the indignities of the electronic computer. With this thought to comfort me—and a deep sigh of relief —I close this chapter.

chapter 3

FLIGHT

Why do angels have wings? Perhaps the early literature of the church provides well-reasoned ecclesiastical explanations, but to my mind the answer is quite simple: The wings of the angel are a symbol of man's eternal yearning to flee his two-dimensional habitat and soar across the heavens above the earth or, like Icarus, on through space to the sun and stars.

What concept of Heaven could be more delightfully desirable than to sever our earthly chains, not only spiritually for our minds and souls, but physically for our bodies as well!

Perhaps, too, it is our suppressed desire to fly that explains the great popularity of bird study as an extracurricular occupation. The appeal, I would guess, lies less in scientific inquiry than in envy. I suspect that every bird watcher has said to himself at one time or another (as I must confess I have), "If I had Aladdin's lamp and a single wish—off I would fly." What a delight it would be!

At any rate, flight has fascinated men throughout history, and many have tried it with little success. To be sure, recent generations have conquered the sky, and it is thrilling to cover great distances in an instant of time. But flying for most of us consists only of sitting still and gazing reflectively out the window of our airborne cabin. We do not experience the exaltation of the wind rushing past our bodies or the excitement of propelling ourselves high above the clouds.

One can imagine only dimly what it would be like to fly through the air under one's own power. The closest I have come to that experience was during an excursion in an aqualung under the surface of the Mediterranean. I could not, of course, soar, glide or dive; I could, in fact, scarcely exceed a walking pace no matter how fiercely I paddled my feet or waved my hands. I was, however, for the first time able to move freely in three dimensions. I could go as I pleased—up or down, forward or backward, to left or to right. It was a magnificent feeling—one almost of liberation. What the fish may have thought of me I can't say, but I am very sure that no aquarium can reproduce the thrill of meeting a fish face to face in his own environment.

Flying is another matter entirely and I must, I suppose, resign myself to the impossibility of personal experience. I can only observe the grace of gull or tern, admire the titmouse as it flies through an opening narrower than its spread wings, marvel at the extraordinary maneuverability of the hummingbird. I can also try to understand, as best I can, how the trick is done.

This brings me finally and perhaps all too slowly to the subject of this chapter. Here I propose to set down what I have learned of the flight technique of birds and particularly of hummingbirds. Many of the data are my own; much has been borrowed from other experimenters. If I do not give credit where credit is due, my omissions are only to make the narrative flow easily and understandably.

Perhaps the most sensible beginning is to describe the anatomy of the wing and its associated muscles. The skeleton of a wing is much like that of a human arm, its parts corresponding to the shoulder joint, upper arm, elbow, forearm, wrist and hand. Feathers are attached to each segment: the *primaries,* or principal flight feathers, to the part representing the hand (though most birds have far more feathers than the hand has fingers), the *secondaries* to the forearm and the *tertiaries* (if any) to the upper arm.

All birds except the hummingbird articulate their wings at shoulder, elbow and wrist. The wing can be extended so that its leading edge from shoulder to thumb, so to speak, is a straight line—it also can bend or fold at elbow and wrist and does so during each wing beat. The rudiments of a folded wing are evident, in fact, with every roast chicken which comes to table. Hand, forearm and upper arm are clearly visible, and even the unskilled carver can dissect out the various parts.

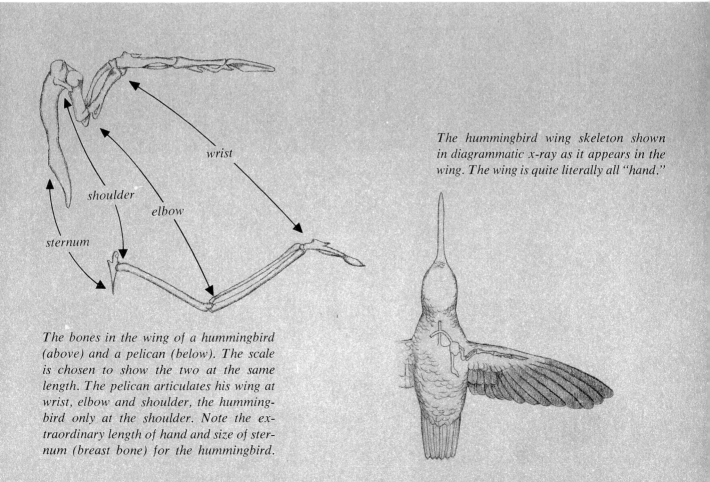

wrist

shoulder

elbow

sternum

The hummingbird wing skeleton shown in diagrammatic x-ray as it appears in the wing. The wing is quite literally all "hand."

The bones in the wing of a hummingbird (above) and a pelican (below). The scale is chosen to show the two at the same length. The pelican articulates his wing at wrist, elbow and shoulder, the hummingbird only at the shoulder. Note the extraordinary length of hand and size of sternum (breast bone) for the hummingbird.

For the hummingbird we have a quite different arrangement; its wing is quite literally all hand. Upper arm and forearm are very short. Elbow and wrist cannot articulate and upper arm and forearm take the shape of a V attached to the shoulder at one side and to the hand at the other. The permanently bent elbow gives it a rigid structure that can articulate freely and in all directions only at the shoulder joint. Curiously it is this combination of rigidity at the elbow and mobility at the shoulder that leads to the unusual efficiency and maneuverability of these birds.

For insect wings not even the vestiges of upper arm and forearm remain, if indeed they were ever present. Insect wings are essentially thin plates articulated only at the shoulder. They move much like the wings of hummingbirds and the flight techniques are closely similar.

For any flying creature, flight, particularly flapping flight, is a process requiring a considerable expenditure of energy. Birds have, as a result, large and well developed flight muscles. The muscles of strong flyers may range from 15 to 25 per cent of the total weight of the bird. For birds less apt to take to the air, such as those which have long been domesticated, the flight muscles tend to atrophy somewhat and to decrease in size. A chicken, as anyone with a barnyard background can attest, flaps its wings more for show than for flight, and wing muscles represent only 6 to 7 per cent of its weight.

The hummingbird flight muscles comprise 25 to 30 per cent of total body weight, more than those of any other bird. As the wing moves, a "depressor" muscle powers the downbeat and an "elevator" muscle the upbeat, the depressor outweighing the elevator by a factor of two. In most other birds the elevator muscle is relatively much smaller. In the stronger flyers, for example, it is one-tenth or even as little as one-twentieth the weight of the depressor muscle.

Since muscle energy is certainly related to muscle weight, the hummingbird must derive power during upbeat as well as downbeat. Other birds, on the other hand, derive little or no power as the wings move upward. Forward speed, lift, and maneuverability come only from the powerful down thrust.

A hummingbird is much like a helicopter in its flight performance. To be sure, the wings go backward and forward, more like the oars of a boat than the circular whirl of the helicopter rotor. The effect, however, is much the same. If a helicopter hovers, the rotor is in a plane parallel to the earth's surface—so are the wings of a hummingbird. As the helicopter moves forward or backward, the rotor tilts in the appropriate direction—so do the wings of a hummingbird. The helicopter can rise directly from a given spot without a runway for take-off —so can a hummingbird.

By contrast, ordinary birds are more akin to conventional aircraft. They cannot hover or fly backward—they are limited to forward flight. Not all require a runway for take-off, but they do need an "assist" in one way or another. Small birds such as the chickadee use the spring in their legs to launch themselves into the air at minimum flying velocity—ducks and other water birds paddle their feet and flap their wings to build up to take-off speed. The larger land birds run and flap until they can become airborne.

All birds seem to have a constant speed motor, which is to say that their wing beat rate does not vary. I have taken several hundred high speed motion pictures of the female ruby throat and it is clear that the wing frequency varies not more than 5 per cent whether the bird is hovering, flying forward or backward, flying at maximum velocity, or maneuvering for a quick getaway. To be sure, the wing beat rate varies with the individual, but for the average female the wings beat 52 times per second no matter what the bird is doing. My data for other species of hummingbirds and for ordinary birds are much more limited but the evidence indicates that wing beat rate is constant for any individual whether it weighs a fraction of an ounce like the ruby-crowned kinglet or the 10 pounds of the majestic golden eagle.

After much observation and study, it occurred to me that the constancy of wing beat rate could be very neatly rationalized by applying the well-developed theory for mechanical oscillators. The most universally familiar device of this type is the pendulum of a "grandfather" clock. The pendulum has a "natural frequency," which depends solely on its length. The length is chosen to give a natural frequency of one full beat per second. If the bearing from which the pendulum is suspended were truly frictionless, if we were to eliminate air resistance and disconnect the clock mechanism, the pendulum would continue to swing indefinitely at its natural frequency and we would have a form of perpetual motion. In a real clock, no one of these assumptions is valid, and the sum of the three forces—bearing friction, air resistance, and clock drive—decreases or "damps" the amplitude of the pendulum's swing. The frequency remains unchanged and the pendulum will continue to beat once per second with steadily decreasing amplitude until it finally comes to rest.

Unless we were willing to stand by and give the pendulum a shove now and then to keep it oscillating, our clock would run for only a few minutes. In the clock this "shove" is provided by the weights, which slowly descend over a period of hours or days and then are cranked up again to renew the cycle. We do indeed give the pendulum an occasional push, but the action of the weights limits the necessity of human aid to tolerable intervals.

The "shove" given to the pendulum must for greatest efficiency be synchronized with its natural frequency. To make this a bit clearer we might transfer our scene of operations from the pendulum of a clock to a child in a swing. A moment's reflection will show that a child in a swing is simply a pendulum in another form. The suspending rope is the rod, the child and swing are the weight, the friction of the suspension and air resistance produce the damping, and the driving force which keeps the assembly in motion is, inevitably and unfortunately, you. Pull the child back and push him forward and he will oscillate happily at the natural frequency of the assembly. Should you be unfeeling enough then to walk away, the amplitude of the swing will decrease (its frequency remaining unchanged) until it comes to rest and you must face a child motionless and indignant. Should you become reconciled to duty and give the child a proper ride, note that you must supply the small push at precisely the point at which your human pendulum reaches the top of its stroke. If you push at a frequency faster or slower than the natural frequency of the swing, you will wear yourself out and your small customer will have a rough and unrewarding experience.

For all mechanical oscillators, there are four factors that describe their motion:

1. The weight and length of the oscillating systems — viz: The weight of the child, the length of the rope.

2. The restoring force which tends to bring the oscillator to neutral position. For child and swing, this is the force of gravity.

3. The damping resistance which the oscillator must overcome. This is principally the bearing friction at the point of suspension of the swing, plus the air resistance of the assembly.

4. The driving force, which overcomes the damping resistance and keeps the oscillator moving at the desired amplitude. This is provided by your pushes for the child in the swing.

To return now to the flying animals—insects, hummingbirds, other birds—the oscillating system is made up of the wings, wing muscles and some part of the animal skeleton. The restoring force is due to the elasticity of the muscle tissue, which acts much as a rubber band would act, i.e., the more it is stretched the more force it exerts to bring itself back to the unstretched condition. The damping resistance is due to internal friction and to the aerodynamic work done by the wings to keep the animal in the air and moving forward. The driving force arises out of the conversion of food to muscle energy through the chemistry of the animals' metabolic processes.

The wing beat rate—the natural frequency of the system—depends only on the first two factors, the dimensions and weight of the oscillating system and the restoring force, or elasticity of the muscle. For maximum efficiency the driving force, necessary to overcome the damping resistance, must be applied at this natural frequency. This is why wing beat rate is in general independent of the aerodynamic demand.

For large birds, in which wing beat rates are sufficiently low to permit visual observation, we can see that the birds decrease the amplitude of the wing beat as the flying effort eases. A pelican, for example, flying down wind seems almost to glide and the angle through which the wings move decreases to a low value. Should the bird climb, or turn to fly up wind, the amplitude increases with the added aerodynamic demand. The wing frequency, however, remains constant.

Occasionally a bird will greatly increase its aerodynamic effort —when braking for a landing, for example, or when attempting to elude a predator. Here we see the wing beat rate increase temporarily, since the aerodynamic gain is greater than the loss in efficiency from increasing wing frequency above the "natural" value. The inordinate increase in muscular effort can be sustained for the briefest of intervals.

I could at this point set down a series of long and complicated equations derived from oscillator theory that would support the points just made. I suspect, however, that most readers will be far happier without them and perhaps even willing to take my word for the validity of what has been said. I can, however, present one more analogy that shows the importance of synchronizing driving force with the natural frequency of the oscillator.

I was taught as a boy that when walking with a lady, good manners required that I "keep step." If the lady were petite, I would find myself in considerable difficulty—her natural pace being much more rapid than mine, adjustment for any extended period became almost painful.
With apologies for a comparison that may seem unchivalrous, her

oscillating system was shorter and less massive than mine, hence her "natural frequency" greater. Shortening my pace to hers, i.e., putting my driving force out of synchronism with my own natural frequency, required far more muscular effort on my part than if I had thrown politeness to the winds and used my natural gait.

It is interesting to note how oscillator theory works out for the whole sweep of flying animals, from, let us say, a gnat at one end of the scale to a swan at the other. First, however, I must say a word or two about the principles of dimensional similarity.

We all remember "Alice in Wonderland" and the bottle she encountered labeled "Drink me." When she followed instructions she did indeed shrink to Lilliputian size, remaining, however, "dimensionally similar" in all respects to her normal self. This simply means that if she were reduced to one-tenth her original height, the length of her arms, or fingers or nose would also be one-tenth normal. Thus, for any dimensionally similar series of animals ranging in size from the very small to the very large, all linear dimensions should vary in the same ratio—all areas should vary with the square of any linear dimension, and all volumes or weights with the cube of a linear dimension.

Applying oscillator theory to a series of flying animals, we establish a very simple relationship requiring the product of wing beat rate (f) and any linear dimension—the length of wing, for example—(l) to be constant, or to state it in mathematical terms:

$$fl = a \; constant.$$

There are enough data for insects and birds to test the hypothesis. When we do so we find it very slightly in error. The data appear to show that for all flying animals frequency decreases somewhat less rapidly than the formula for increasing wing length would indicate. The actual situation is about as follows:

$$fl^{1.15} = a \; constant.$$

The explanation appears to lie in the fact that thickness of the wing increases somewhat faster than its length, hence the weight of the wing as the flyer increases in size varies not with the cube, but with some higher power (3.3–3.5) of the length.

I suspect that Nature has a sound reason for this departure from dimensional similarity, perhaps to take care of the necessity of increasing the stiffness of a long wing to keep it from cracking or breaking under the strain of flight. In any event, it is a striking tribute to Nature's consistency that we can start with a gnat—wing length 7 millimeters and wing beat rate 500 per second—and with our formula predict accurately that a mute swan with a wing length 100 times as great will beat its wings 1.5 times per second.

A more persuasive demonstration of Nature's adherence to the principles of dimensional similarity is evident when we plot the weight of flying animals against their wing length in logarithmic coordinates. On such a plot we see that for the whole sweep of flying things—from a gnat weighing a milligram to a swan weighing ten million times as much—the weight varies approximately as the cube of the wing length. This does not mean that a gnat increased ten million times in size (which Heaven forbid) would even remotely resemble a swan. It merely defines a general relationship between two physical attributes.

In the figure it is clear from the "scatter" of the many points that Nature's model permits quite radical departures from the average. No one would recognize any great degree of similarity between bee and butterfly, mosquito and beetle, or, among birds, between swift and crow. Neither are they "dimensionally similar" in the sense of our figure. It is only when one takes a broad look at the whole family of flyers that the underlying dimensional relationships become apparent.

The wing length in all cases is measured from wing tip to the first articulated joint. For insects and hummingbirds this is the whole wing since the first articulated joint is at the shoulder. For other birds the first joint is at the wrist and the length of the whole wing is almost twice

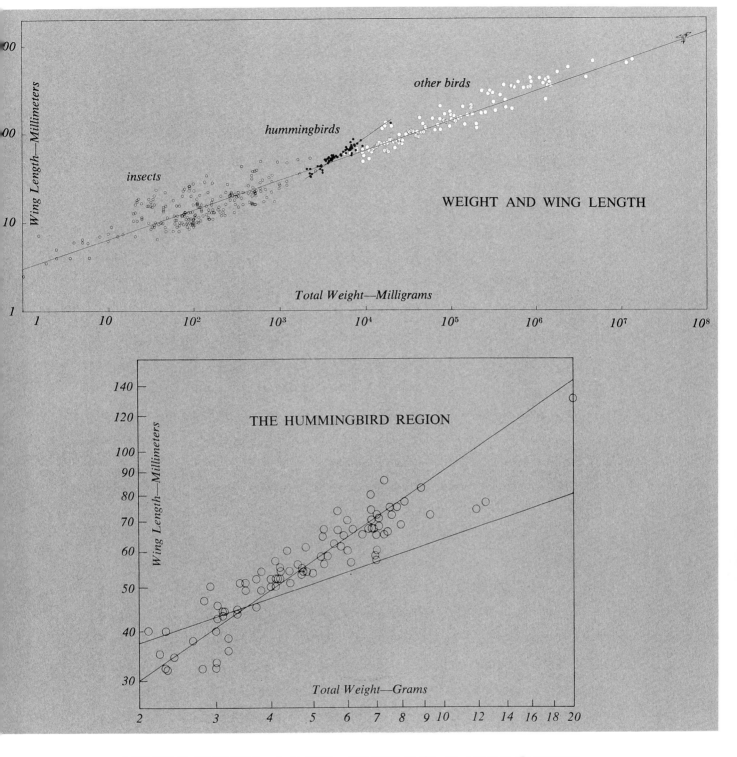

WEIGHT AND WING LENGTH

The upper chart is what might be called a "gnat to condor" curve showing in logarithmic coordinates the relationship between wing length and total weight for the whole range of flying animals. The slope of the line is 3, which means simply that the body weight is proportional to the cube of the wing length. The hummingbirds fall almost exactly at the center, midway between insects and other birds. At upper right is our hypothetical angel or more precisely, a point on the line representing the weight of a human body which produces a wing length (wrist to tip) of about four feet. The relatively greater scatter for insects demonstrates Nature's virtuosity in designing a widely differing array of flying animals at the small end of the scale.

The lower chart is an enlarged segment of the center of the "gnat to condor" line. The points plotted represent only hummingbirds. The steep slope of the hummingbird line shows the anomalous weight—wing length relationship. For hummingbirds W is proportional to $l^{3/2}$, for other birds to l^3. The lone point at upper right is for **P**. gigas, the largest hummingbird. Note its position among the swifts and swallows in upper diagram.

the "tip to wrist" dimension. It is odd that the correlation between weight and wing length for other birds should nonetheless be consistent with the data for insects and hummingbirds. Perhaps when Nature introduced three points of articulation (shoulder, elbow and wrist) she made corresponding changes in wing geometry and aerodynamic behavior so as to retain dimensional similarity with other flyers.

And now, what of the hummingbirds' place in this grand roster? The fact is that they fall almost exactly midway in the catalog of flying animals. Their weight is roughly five thousand times that of our small gnat, and one five-thousandth that of the mute swan. It is difficult to see why this should be so, but I feel quite certain that the answer is not pure coincidence. Nature is far too purposeful to act at random.

Note also that for the hummingbirds Nature has changed her structural model. Instead of the weight increasing with the cube, it increases with the three-halves power of the wing length. Since insects, hummingbirds and other birds all overlap into their respective size ranges, it is obvious that there could have been no *a priori* reason for a model change in the hummingbird area. Even so, the number of insects and other birds found in the hummingbird size range is relatively small, and the hummingbirds may in effect represent an area of transition between birds and insects.

Some data on the overlapping may be interesting. The smallest hummingbird, *Calypte helenae*, weighs 2 grams or a bit less. There is a "sphinx" moth, also an excellent flyer, which weighs a bit more, about 2.3 grams. There are, moreover, some monstrous beetles, of which the largest, aptly called *Goliathus goliathus*, weighs between 35 and 40 grams. This is well past the largest hummingbird, *Patagona gigas*, which weighs a mere 20 grams. There are many birds, in fact, lighter than our giant beetle, which actually weighs as much as a bluebird or catbird. The smallest may well be *Regulus regulus*, a tiny kinglet weighing 3.8 grams, well down among the smaller hummingbirds. *Goliathus* can fly, after

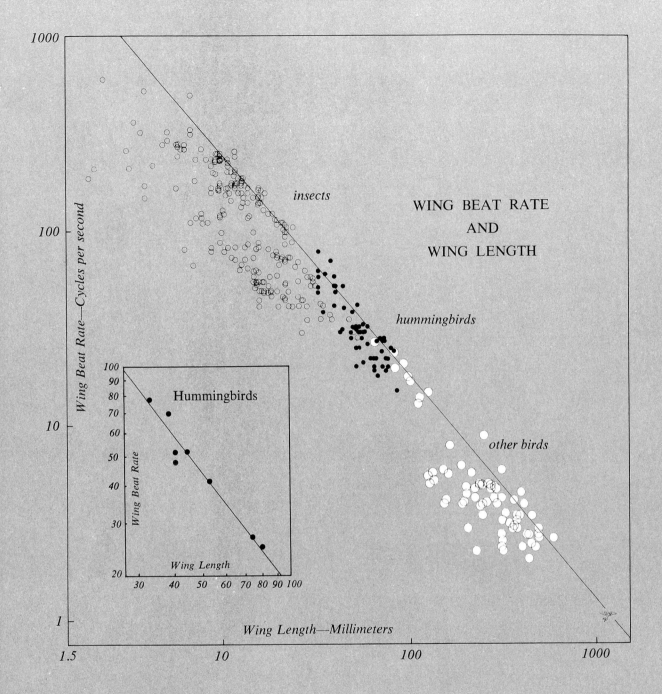

WING BEAT RATE AND WING LENGTH

Here we have another "gnat to condor" line, this one on the relationship between wing length and wing beat rate. The slope of the boundary line is 1.15, which means that the apparent limit for the relationship is defined by the equation $fl^{1.15} = 3540$. The insects, as in the curve on page 213, show a considerable scatter. The animals represented by points far to the left of the boundary line are poor flyers, those close to the line are much more proficient. Our hypothetical angel (note at lower right) would beat his or her wings at a rate of once per second.

The insert shows the hummingbird region, the values here determined more precisely from high speed motion pictures. The slope is 1.25, somewhat greater than that for the gnat to condor boundary. The rationale for the hummingbird anomaly is given in the text.

a fashion, but in comparison with his "other bird" neighbors he is clumsy and slow, an entomological tortoise to an avian hare.

Extension of the hummingbird model into the insect or "other bird" areas is limited, however, for any substantial liberties would produce some startling aerodynamic monstrosities. A hypothetical hummingbird with a weight equal to that of the mute swan would have a wing 32 feet long—manifestly an absurdity. At the other end of the scale, a gnat on the hummingbird model weighing a milligram would have wings so short that a microscope would be needed even to see them. The wing length would be less than one one-hundredth of an inch and the wings would have to beat 20,000 times per second!

I think the "transition" hypothesis is best, since the hummingbird model could not have been used for anything more than a fraction of the span embraced in the catalog of flying animals. (The weight of hummingbirds ranges from two to twenty grams, a factor of ten; for the span of all flying things, the range is nearly a hundred million.) A flight technique which in the hummingbird size range is graceful and easy would become clumsy, even preposterous, if extended far outside it.

We come now to the aerodynamics of bird flight or, in simpler terms, how beating wings generate the forces that supply lift and propulsion. I doubt that many subjects have been studied more assiduously or over so long a period of years. Aristotle (385-322 B.C.) was the first to write extensively on flight. He was followed by a host of others, whose names alone would fill a small volume. One energetic gentleman has recently compiled a list of over 2000 titles of publications dealing with animal flight, and doubtless there are many more.

Unfortunately, all of the experiments and speculations have produced little real understanding of the subject. Some observers, after years of study and the development of complex mathematical formulae, have even concluded that it is quite impossible for birds and insects (or man for that matter) to become airborne.

The development of modern aircraft got little assistance from the many studies of bird and insect flight. Success came eventually from an attack *de novo* using rigid airfoils and whirling propellers. No successful large-scale machine has been built that flaps its wings. Von Holst and Küchemann,* to be sure, constructed flying models called ornithopters, which had remarkable stability and performance. These authors maintained stoutly that such "powered wing" aircraft had great possibilities either in their own right or as a means to the improvement of conventional machines. Nothing practical, I regret to say, has emerged from their studies.

The analytical problem in defining the forces acting on the wing of a bird is indeed formidable. The wings of modern aircraft are rigid, built to a definite profile, and can be tested fully in wind tunnels. Propellers and helicopter rotors are fixed in their geometrical relationships and their performance also can be readily analyzed and predicted.

A bird's wing, on the other hand, is a completely flexible airfoil. The leading edge, formed by the bones of upper arm, forearm and wrist, is rigid, but the feathers forming the surface of the wing twist and bend under the action of the wind. The angle of attack of the wing, so important in appraising aerodynamic performance, will vary from shoulder to tip, and the resulting twist will be different not only for downbeat as compared with upbeat, but will change during every instant of the complete wing beat.

The resulting complexity of motion simply does not lend itself to detailed analysis. Perhaps with modern electronic computers something might be done, but until that very great effort is made, we shall have to rest content with our imperfect and rudimentary knowledge.

At first impression, the flight of hummingbirds seems to present a simple case. The wings, articulated only at the shoulder, more or less resemble a pair of flat paddles. In high speed motion pictures, their wings seem to be "rowing" them through the air, and superficially it

*Von Holst's classical paper in the Journal für Ornithologie, October 1943, gives detailed directions for the construction of such models. Any reader sufficiently inspired can, if he wishes and has sufficient fortitude, attempt the construction of a full-scale version.

appears that aerodynamic analysis should not be difficult. Unfortunately the problem turns out to be extremely complex — far too complex for me to cope with—and I am forced to limit myself here to a few observations derived primarily from high-speed motion pictures.

There is, however, one rather pretty bit of analysis that can be made for hummingbirds in hovering flight. We recall that these birds are anomalous in the sense that their weight varies as the three-halves power of their wing length. (For all other birds, and for insects, the weight varies as l^3.)

Stated in mathematical terms, the theory of mechanical oscillators as applied to birds requires that f^2 be proportional to bl^2/l^5 where f is the wing beat rate, l the length of wing, and b a linear dimension of the wing muscle, proportional in turn to a linear dimension of the body.

Since we know that the weight of the bird, proportional to the cube of a bodily dimension, is in turn proportional to $l^{3/2}$, then b should be proportional to $l^{1/2}$. Substituting for b in the above equation we find that $fl^{5/4}$ should be constant.

Turning now to the aerodynamics of hovering flight we know that the weight of the bird must be balanced exactly by the upward force of the rising air column produced by the beating wings. Expressed mathematically, W, the weight of the bird, should be proportional to l^4f^2. Substituting $l^{3/2}$ for W, we find again that $fl^{5/4}$ should be constant.

Note that we have arrived at the conclusion that $fl^{5/4}$ is constant from two distinct and unrelated principles—oscillator theory and the aerodynamics of hovering flight.

I have measured wing beat rate and wing length for forty or more hummingbird species ranging from *Calliphlox amethystina* ($f = 80$, $l = 33$ mm.) to *Patagona gigas* ($f = 10$, $l = 135$ mm.) and, lo and behold, we find experimentally that $fl^{5/4}$ is indeed constant.

I am afraid, however, that in spite of this minor experimental and analytical triumph, the result is not of too much significance. It is broadly valid for the hummingbird model, but cannot be translated to insects and other birds.

Turning from theory to experiment, I have attempted to establish factual information on two points: First, the change in the aspect of the wing beat as the forward velocity of the bird increased and, second, the maximum flying speed of which these small birds were capable.

To do this, I needed first of all a high-speed motion picture camera of a very special type. Many such cameras are commercially available, but unfortunately all require an appreciable time (a half second or so) to reach full speed. Since within this interval the bird would long since have departed, some new method had to be devised to insure an instantaneous start; that is, to have the film accelerate from zero to 1500 frames per second in not more than a few thousandths of a second.

Starting from scratch and with much kindly assistance, a concept was finally evolved and a version we called "Mark I" was constructed. The successful result is neither elegant nor compact, and I doubt that Eastman or Bell and Howell would find it a marketable product, but it does start instantly, permits film speeds up to 1500 frames per second and can be triggered by interruption of a beam of light shining on a photocell. (With this device the birds become their own photographers.)

A second problem was to devise a method that would induce the birds to fly at various controlled forward velocities, from zero to the top speed of which they were capable. This required a bit of doing, and after many tries, I almost gave up in disgust. Fortunately, inspiration finally came, and the solution turned out to be quite simple.

The principle employed was not unlike that of a treadmill. Again with much kind assistance, a wind tunnel was constructed about eighteen inches in diameter with a powerful fan at one end. The fan's output could be varied to produce a head wind of any required velocity. A feeder was placed at the exit end of the tunnel, its spout centered in the air stream. A bird coming in to feed, confronted with a head wind of any given velocity, would perform precisely as though he were himself flying at a similar speed, although his position with respect to feeder (and camera) would remain stationary. The wings, in other words, assume the same position they would take if the bird were flying in still air at a velocity equal to that of the air blowing through the tunnel.

Camera, tunnel and fan, and the electronic equipment to produce a flash for each frame on the film must have presented an awesome aspect to a tiny hummingbird looking for an easy meal. My children, lacking their father's thirst for scientific knowledge, speedily christened the setup "Daddy's Torture Chamber."

I hasten here to plead "not guilty" to torture, for the birds seemed actually to enjoy the challenge. With the noisy fan going at full blast, the buzz of the camera affected them scarcely at all, and at high wind velocities they seemed almost to make a game of it.

The equipment was completed and successfully tested during August, at which time the young were out of the nest and vying with their mothers for a chance at the feeder. It was amusing here to note the difference between the wisdom of maturity and the brashness of youth. The adult females soon learned to line themselves up with the feeder about eight to ten feet downstream from the exit of the wind tunnel. They would then work their way in fits and starts until the goal was achieved. The impatient young would fly diagonally up into the wind stream only to be blown head over heels when they encountered the full blast. But under mother's tutelage they soon learned the trick and were finally taking nourishment with as much aplomb as their parent.

Unfortunately, transfer of such a complex apparatus to the hinterlands of Brazil or Ecuador seemed impractical and, even had it been attempted, the chance of an adequate power supply seemed remote. These experiments have been limited, therefore, to the hummingbirds found in Delaware, and the data all pertain to the female ruby throat and a miscellaneous collection of offspring.

(*Text continued on page 143*)

FLIGHT...

Wing Patterns and Flight Maneuvers...

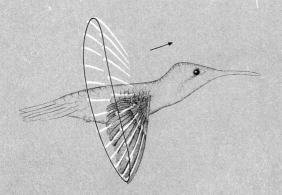

FORWARD 26 MILES PER HOUR
(Top Speed)

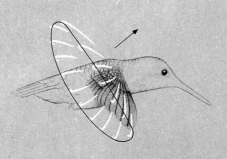

FORWARD 8.6 MILES PER HOUR

HOVERING

BACKWARD FLIGHT

HUMMINGBIRD
WING PATTERNS

FULL
SPEED
AHEAD

Here the bird is flying against a wind velocity of 26 miles per hour, within a mile per hour or so of its top speed. The plane in which the wings beat is now nearly vertical. On the downbeat, the wing tip travels in nearly a straight line. On the upbeat, the wings describe an arc so that the wing tip during the entire cycle moves through a more or less flattened ellipse. While lift is provided in both down- and upbeats, forward thrust seems to be limited to the downbeat. The time interval between successive drawings shown is again two milliseconds.

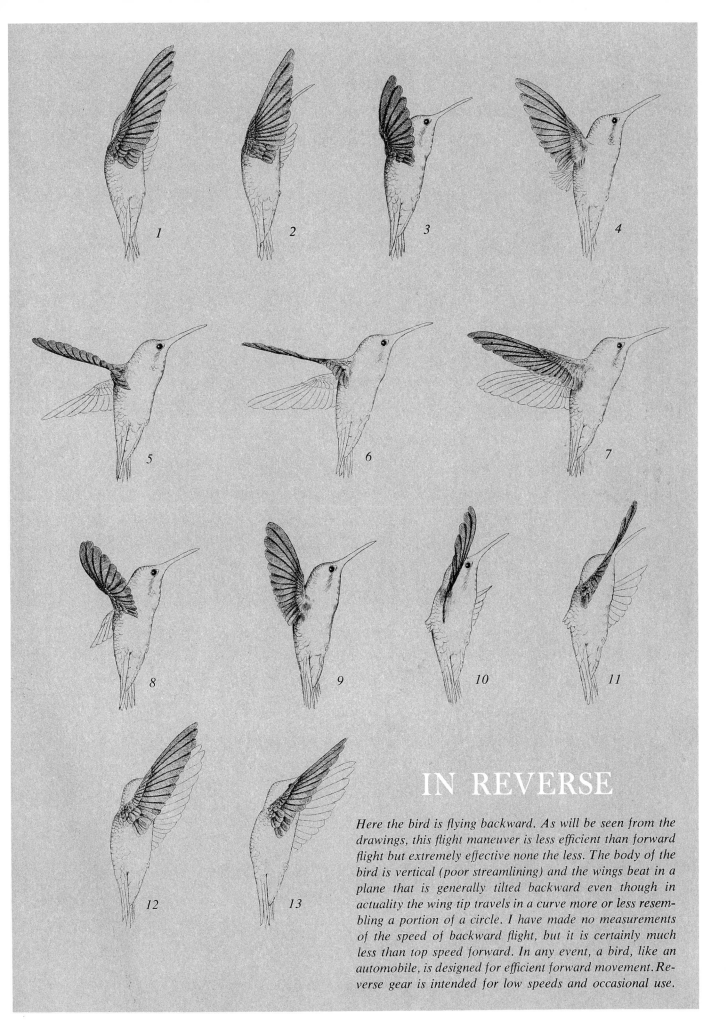

IN REVERSE

Here the bird is flying backward. As will be seen from the drawings, this flight maneuver is less efficient than forward flight but extremely effective none the less. The body of the bird is vertical (poor streamlining) and the wings beat in a plane that is generally tilted backward even though in actuality the wing tip travels in a curve more or less resembling a portion of a circle. I have made no measurements of the speed of backward flight, but it is certainly much less than top speed forward. In any event, a bird, like an automobile, is designed for efficient forward movement. Reverse gear is intended for low speeds and occasional use.

BREAKAWAY

A ruby throat, alarmed, quits the premises

At upper left the bird is feeding peacefully. Startled by the buzz of the high-speed camera (her reaction time is about 20 milliseconds) she spreads her tail and gives a strong forward scoop. At the same time she puts her wings in reverse, thus pulling the beak out of the feeding spout, then rotating her body until in positions 6 and 7 she is virtually flying on her back. She finally performs a roll to get her body right side up and darts away. Note that in 11 and 12 her wings are in position for "full speed ahead" departure. The whole sequence shown here takes place in about two-tenths of a second.

1

2

3

The beginning of the upbeat.
The wings are close to the
body, the elbow and wrist so
positioned that the wings hang
in a nearly vertical plane.

4

5

The midpoint of the powerful
downbeat. Wing surface is at
a maximum, the primaries
strongly curved by pressure of
the air against the feathers.

The primaries during this portion of the upbeat twist on their axis to give a venetian blind effect, so reducing air resistance and minimizing muscular effort to raise the wings. The upbeat produces no lift or propulsion.

10

9

8

7

6

BY WAY OF CONTRAST

A chickadee demonstrates the wing beat of "other birds"

In the powerful down stroke, the primaries are separated and strongly curved due to the pressure of wing against the resisting air. With 6 the up stroke begins. Note that the wing is folded closely into the body. In 7 the primaries twist on their axis to reduce wind resistance. Between 9 and 10 the wing snaps up to its fully extended position to start a new down stroke. The duration of the entire wing beat is 35-40 milliseconds, the upbeat considerably shorter than the downbeat. "Other birds," of which the chickadee is typical, appear to be limited to beating their wings in a vertical plane. Flight control is accomplished by varying the angle of attack of the wings.

HUMMINGBIRD
ACROBATICS

Two years of experimentation and several hundred high-speed sequences give quite conclusive answers to the original questions. Hummingbird flight closely resembles that of a helicopter or, perhaps more accurately, that of the new type of aircraft in which the engines and propellers rotate about a horizontal axis to produce any desired combination of lift and forward thrust.

In hovering flight the wings move backward and forward in a horizontal plane. On the down (or forward) stroke the wing moves with the long leading edge forward, the feathers trailing upward to produce a small positive angle of attack. On the back stroke the leading edge rotates nearly a hundred and eighty degrees and moves backward, the underside of the feathers now uppermost and trailing the leading edge in such a way that the angle of attack varies from wing tip to shoulder, producing a substantial twist in the profile of the wing.

As the velocity increases, the angle of the plane in which the wings beat increases from the horizontal to produce just the proper combination of lift and thrust. At higher and higher velocities the wings beat more and more nearly in a vertical plane. When the vertical position is reached, the birds are at a velocity corresponding to top flying speed.

Top speed for the female ruby throat corresponds to a wind velocity of about 27 miles per hour. When the wind tunnel was boosted to 30 miles per hour, the birds would try repeatedly to reach the feeder. They would enter the wind stream well downstream, fly forward within a tantalizing distance of the feeder only to be unable to make the grade.

It seems clear from these experiments that the top speed of which these birds are capable is something just under 30 miles an hour.

I might add parenthetically that the bees and wasps which normally compete with the hummingbirds at the feeders gave up much earlier. Their top speed seemed scarcely more than ten miles per hour.

While 30 miles per hour seems quite a superb performance for these small birds, the prevailing literature credits them with top speeds up to 60 miles per hour. I think I would bank heavily on the validity of my smaller result. The 60-mile-per-hour figure was obtained, as I understand it, by a man who paced a ruby throat for a short distance with his car. No meteorological data were given, but a tail wind of 30 miles per hour could just account for the difference. At 27 miles per hour my birds were beating their wings in a plane only five degrees from the vertical. It is hard to see how they could have done much more.

Analysis of the high-speed motion pictures produces a few additional bits of information. Perhaps the most important is the constancy of the average wing beat rate, at 53 plus or minus 3 beats per second, irrespective of wind velocity. This led directly to the development of the mechanical oscillator theory discussed earlier in this chapter.

We find also that there is no difference between the duration of the downbeat and that of the upbeat. Each occupies just one half of the full cycle. This result also is in accordance with oscillator theory. The wing, essentially a flat plate, changes neither its weight nor length, hence the same wing beat rate would obtain throughout the cycle.

In a few motion picture sequences at highest wind velocities, we see the bird in the last stages of her approach to the feeder and it is possible to measure the forward distance traveled respectively during downbeat and upbeat. We find in a typical case that the bird advanced on the average 1.6 millimeters during the downbeat, 1.2 millimeters during the upbeat. While 2.8 millimeters per wing beat is only 0.3 miles per hour, remember that the bird was making that headway against a 26 mile per hour wind.

A calculation based on reasonable approximations indicates that the difference between 1.6 and 1.2 millimeters for down and upbeat is about what one might expect if the upbeat produced little or no forward thrust. Hence it is reasonably safe to assume that the downbeat is the principal means of propulsion, at least at these high velocities, whereas it is equally clear that both up- and downbeat contribute to lift.

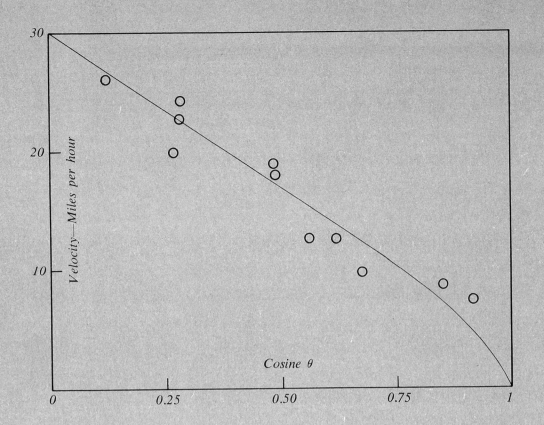

WING PLANE AND WIND VELOCITY

The angle θ is included between a horizontal plane and the plane in which the wings are beating. The velocity is that of the air issuing from the wind tunnel. We can see that the wings assume a more nearly vertical position as the wind velocity increases.

We can also see in slow motion the technique of the fast getaway. When the birds are hovering with the fan turned off, they take fright when the camera starts its buzzing and depart as rapidly as possible. A close study of the film shows, however, that for the duration of a single wing beat nothing happens. Their reaction time then must be about a fiftieth of a second. (Ours by comparison is never less than a tenth of a second, and then only if we happen to be particularly well-coordinated.)

As the first act in the getaway routine, the tail opens and makes a fast forward scoop. Simultaneously the wings assume the position for backward flight. As a result of these two motions, the bird appears to rotate about a horizontal axis until it is flying on its back—feet up, tail toward feeder, head pointed in the opposite direction. The bird then executes a half roll in returning to its normal flying posture and darts off as fast as it can go.

Sometimes, when the bird is not too frightened, it simply backs away from the feeder, giving us the opportunity to observe what happens when the gears go in reverse. Here again the answer is what one might expect. The plane of the wings simply tilts backward, just as with a helicopter rotor, to give a combination of lift and rearward thrust. I did not investigate backward flight quantitatively, but this might have been done by reversing the fan so that it produced suction rather than a blast of air. The thought of a bird being drawn into the fan was too horrible to contemplate, so I contented myself with a few voluntary flight reversals. I could not risk making "Daddy's Torture Chamber" a reality.

It remains now to compare the hummingbird wing beat with that of other birds. For such a comparison it may be as well to take a bird in the hummingbird size range, a chickadee, for example. Here the downbeat is fairly orthodox—upper arm, forearm and wrist are fully extended and together form a rigid leading edge. The feathers are attached to the skeleton in such a way that the wing has a definite camber —a thickened leading edge tapering to a thin trailing edge, the cross section being much like that of the wing of an airplane. Wind resistance causes the outer primaries to curve sharply upward and to separate, each feather tilting toward the wind to form its own angle of attack. In contrast to the hummingbird, chickadees (and other birds) appear to move their wings only in a vertical plane, and vary lift and propulsion by changing the angle of attack of the wing itself.

The upbeat by contrast is quite complex. Flexing the joints at elbow and wrist, the whole wing is folded in close to the body. The elbow is bent, and the primaries from wrist to tip hang in a plane parallel to the body and nearly perpendicular to the ground. For the greater part of the upbeat the individual primary feathers twist on their axis with *146* openings between them to diminish air resistance, the whole effect somewhat resembling an open venetian blind. Finally near the end of the upbeat the wrist flips up, the bent elbow straightens, and the wing is fully extended, ready for the powerful downbeat.

It seems fairly certain that propulsion and probably lift as well are contributed only by the downbeat. Observing the upbeat in slow motion, it is difficult to see how it could possibly contribute to flight. Furthermore, the weights of depressor and elevator muscles are in the ratio of about fifteen to one, hence the elevator muscle can do no more than raise the wing—the much larger depressor muscle must contribute the power for steady flight.

Since the effective length of the wing is greater during downbeat than upbeat, oscillator theory would require a correspondingly greater time interval for the downbeat. Analysis in slow motion of a chickadee in flight shows that this is actually the case, the duration of the two halves of the wing beat having the ratio five to three.

The maximum flying speed of the chickadee is clearly less than that of the hummingbird. Twelve to fifteen miles per hour is the maximum for the former as compared with twenty-five to thirty for the female ruby throat. In maneuverability also the hummingbird comes out on top, with its ability to hover, to fly forward, backward or sideways with the greatest ease. The chickadee, like ordinary aircraft, can only fly forward, and while its aerial acrobatics are truly remarkable, its maneuverability is limited by that circumstance. Perhaps the distinction after all is academic—both birds have extraordinary aerial agility—and in a functional sense lead their airborne existence happily and successfully.

As I write finis to this essay, I conclude that the information is fragmentary and I regret that except for grandfather clocks and children in swings, I have no sweeping aerodynamic theories to propound to explain the flight of hummingbirds, gnats, swans or even that of angels.

As to angels, we can perhaps indulge in a few speculations on their general characteristics. Let's assume first that our angel is flesh and blood and not a disembodied spirit. In size we might select one midway between the masculine and the feminine, weighing perhaps a hundred and fifty pounds.

We cannot admit even the suggestion of an angel with hummingbird characteristics since its wings would be a monstrous 100 feet in length. We can, however, fit our angel into the "other bird" model. The wing from wrist to tip would be about four feet long, its total length between six and seven feet. When folded neatly into the body, the end of the wing would come just below the knee—comfortable enough for perching and walking. The wings would beat about once every second —a nice easy rhythm—not too far from a normal walking pace. The wings would, however, be heavy, perhaps a quarter the weight of the body and, alas, and here lies the rub: The human frame hasn't the pectoral muscles to drive such formidable gear. Human pectorals are barely five per cent of the total body weight and a reasonable aerial job would call for at least fifteen per cent.

But wait a bit! With aluminum, nylon and other materials of high strength, we might manage to build a much lighter wing. And we do have sixteen per cent of our body weight in our leg muscles. If we could only figure out an efficient way to transfer the energy of the legs to a set of new light weight wings!

Well, certainly not for me! But for my great- or great-great or great-great-great grandchildren? Perhaps. It's just barely possible.

chapter 4

METHODS AND EQUIPMENT

"What kind of camera do you use? Does it have a very fast shutter? Don't you need long telephoto lenses?" These and many similar questions bring me finally to this chapter on how my pictures were taken. I don't propose to write it on a "do it yourself" basis. If I did, I should have to present endless wiring diagrams and scale drawings of apparatus and I doubt, furthermore, that there are many enthusiasts likely to set forth in pursuit of these elusive birds with two hundred and fifty pounds of gear. I shall stick to principles, therefore, and let the more intimate details go.

The heart of my equipment, and its most essential and bulky feature, is the apparatus which produces an electronic flash of very short duration. There is no camera shutter fast enough to "stop" a hummingbird wing. This can be done only by using an extremely short and extremely bright flash of light. The electronic equipment available in any camera store has a flash duration of about one-thousandth of a

149

second—far too long for "stop action" photography. In this interval of time, the bird would complete one twentieth of its entire wing beat and a blurred image would result.

It was necessary to start from scratch and to beg, borrow and steal ideas from every fruitful source. I am now using what must be at least "Mark V," having tried and discarded many previous designs. The present equipment comprises three lamps with associated electronic equipment, producing a flash thirty-millionths of a second in duration. The power input to the lamps is 150 watt seconds. To give a better idea of what this power means, a lamp burning continuously at equal brilliance would require 5000 kilowatts.

The flash outfit is battery driven and weighs about thirty pounds. If one thinks that overly heavy, I should add that it took much ingenuity on the part of many people to reduce the weight even to that figure. The camera shutter is a standard item with built-in triggering contacts for the flash unit. In addition to the triggering function, it serves also to *exclude* sunlight. The bird must be illuminated only by the electronic flash. If the shutter is open long enough for daylight to affect the exposure, ghost images of a blurred wing are superimposed on the sharp image produced electronically — a disagreeable result and one which I confess has marred many otherwise pretty pictures.

The camera I prefer is a Hasselblad, although I must add that it has been fairly extensively modified to make it conform to my requirements. I use neither the standard focal plane shutter nor the lens. My lenses are mounted in their own compur type shutter and the focal plane shutter is either disconnected in the open position or locked open for each picture. While many other cameras could be used satisfactorily, the Hasselblad has the advantage of compactness, can be focused directly through the taking lens by means of a mirror reflex device and uses interchangeable film magazines which permit leaving the camera in place without disturbing its orientation or focus.

The focal length of the lens is not at all critical. Since the apparatus is operated remotely, the distance between lens and object has no particular significance. For nearly all of my pictures I have used a lens of 135 millimeter focal length—not a telephoto. There is also no point in a high-speed lens, since in use it is stopped down to a very low aperture. A wide-open aperture of f5.6-8 serves adequately for focusing, and a type of lens chosen for high performance in close-ups is desirable.

Triggering is controlled remotely. The picture can be taken manually, or automatically by the bird interrupting a beam of light shining on a photocell. A solenoid mounted in the cable release socket on the shutter does the actual triggering. An electronic circuit, transistorized for compactness and battery driven, amplifies the pulse from the photocell sufficiently to operate the solenoid. A cord, 50 to 75 feet long, permits the operator to remain at a respectful distance.

It is a curious fact that the birds will tolerate a tremendous array of apparatus—tripod and camera, lamp standards, photocell and flash light, cords running in all directions—without apparently caring a bit. They seem to realize that the apparatus is inanimate and no source of danger. The human operator, however, must remain at an appropriate distance at the end of a long control cord, the distance depending on the timidity of the particular bird.

Another critical point is the time interval between the interruption of the light beam by the bird and the actual taking of the picture. This must be very short. Birds in flight move rapidly and could, if this point were not met, fly out of focus before the flash takes the picture. This is another reason for using a compur shutter, and a high voltage pulse to the solenoid. The resulting time interval is about a fortieth of a second—fast enough for the great majority of cases.

One could, of course, be sporting and trigger the camera manually. Unfortunately, my reaction time is well over a tenth of a second, hence manual triggering for me usually results in pictures of the tail of a departing bird or no picture at all. The photocell does much better and I am quite happy to use it and admit my failings.

The apparatus I have described requires the operator to go to the camera each time a picture is taken to advance the film and recock the shutter. Under certain circumstances this becomes rather a nuisance, for at each human approach the birds take flight, and require a substantial time interval to assure themselves that the bad man has gone away.

This disadvantage has been overcome in a recent model by motorizing the camera and hooking the motor into the electronic circuit so that every time the flash goes off the motor advances the film another frame. The compur shutter is also modified by removing nearly all its innards, leaving only the "bulb" setting. The solenoid in this case is pulsed in such a way that the shutter opens just enough to trigger the flash contacts; the pulse then is dissipated (a suitable combination of voltage, capacitance and resistance does the trick) and the shutter spring closes the shutter. With this device the operator need not go near the equipment until a whole roll of film has been exposed. For nesting birds, or in fact for any timid bird, this is a real boon—in effect it permits at least twice the number of pictures in a given time interval.

A word might be said about film format. I use Ektachrome film of the 120 size with pictures 2¼ inches square. I strongly recommend this format over the more conventional 35 millimeter color film. The point is that when one takes pictures of flying birds, they do not pose prettily in the center of the picture, but may be "caught" in any one of the four corners of the film. Such transparencies are not very pretty since no one is esthetically satisfied by a projected picture with the bird off in one corner. With the larger film size this difficulty can be neatly overcome by composing the picture with a pair of scissors and mounting the resultant segment of the original film in a standard 2 by 2 mount with an appropriate mask. As an added advantage, there is currently a greater array of color film types available in the 120 than in the

35 millimeter size. Finally, for maximum detail one needs the largest possible image, and the large format is a clear gain when the inherent film definition is on the low side.

We come finally to the disagreeable problem of insuring adequate depth of field, to be certain that all parts of the flying bird will be in focus. As every photographer knows, depth of field decreases geometrically as the size of the object approaches the size of the image. For small hummingbirds, taken at an object-to-film reduction of three, the problem becomes really acute. Since one has limited control over the birds, the only solution is to use a very small lens aperture, and here I have standardized on f32. This requires the flash lamps very close to the subject—twelve to fifteen inches in actual practice—in order to secure adequate illumination. Fortunately, after the first two or three exposures, the birds seem not to mind either the proximity of the lamps or the brilliant flash. I can't imagine what they think is happening—perhaps an unexpected flash of lightning, which they probably experience regularly. In any event, they seem quite happy to accommodate themselves to the photographer's requirements.

All of this equipment, as I have said, is heavy and, since I travel with two complete set-ups, to say nothing of innumerable spares, it adds up to about two hundred and fifty pounds. I have found it prudent, particularly when traveling in Latin America, to carry it all along as personal baggage, which means in effect that there are three of us traveling, my wife and I and another full passage worth of excess baggage. On a trip to Ecuador on which my wife and I were traveling tourist, the equipment, due to the vagaries of excess baggage charges, was traveling first class. When I suggested to the stewardess that I might have the free drink to which my baggage was entitled, she showed no sympathy. My baggage, it seemed, wasn't thirsty or at least not vocally so, and my drink would be 50 cents, please!

The weight and bulk of the equipment quite obviously prevent my chasing after the birds in the field. It is therefore essential to devise some means of persuading the birds to come to the equipment. This in turn requires an attraction sufficiently enticing to overcome the disadvantages of cords, apparatus and artificial bolts of lightning. I have found only two such lures—food and an occupied nest.

For hummingbirds the nest is good only for pictures of the female. The male, as I have said previously, has nothing to do with nest construction, incubation, or care of the young. Food on the other hand is a sufficiently strong magnet for both sexes, to say nothing of their offspring and a miscellaneous collection of competing insects.

The only difficulty here is that the birds take some time to get used to an artificial nectar supply. One must either arrange a visit with someone who feeds hummingbirds regularly or find a cooperative soul willing to set out and service feeders for a month or two before our arrival, so that when we appear on the scene the birds are used to the feeders and need only accustom themselves to us. Fortunately, hummingbirds are as attracted to an easy meal as most vertebrates, including man. Once the feeders are in operation and the birds locate them, they are most reluctant to go back to their flower-by-flower approach.

A fair number of hummingbird species simply will not come voluntarily to an artificial food supply. The only solution here is to capture the birds, keep them for a time in cages, accustom them to a sugar-water diet and finally photograph them in captivity. I would guess that about half the birds in the present portfolio were photographed in this way.

It may be amusing and edifying to describe some of the techniques I have seen used for capturing these little birds alive.

The most sporting method was that used by a gentleman in Ecuador. His weapon was a blow gun—precisely the type used by the Ecuadorian Indians to obtain food in the jungle. The Indian, however, uses poisoned darts when in pursuit of wild game, whereas my friend's ammunition consisted only of water-softened clay pellets. He was skillful enough to draw a bead on an unsuspecting hummingbird and to hit it just hard enough to stun it, but to leave it otherwise unharmed. Then it was merely a matter of picking the bird up and popping it into a cage, whereupon it would soon recover, indignant but none the worse for wear. He could get his bird at a range up to 25 or 30 feet. If you think this is easy—try it some time.

Dr. Ruschi's method, as I observed it, was almost as spectacular. He used what resembled a collapsible fly casting rod extensible to a maximum length of thirty feet. The last segment of the rod was a section of bamboo about a sixteenth of an inch in diameter. This he smeared with a "gacky" substance made by boiling linseed oil for many hours. He would stand with this contraption extended over a flowering shrub, wait for a bird to appear and then flick the tip deftly across the bird's back. Stuck fast to the adhesive, the bird could then be hauled in and carefully detached. When, as sometimes happened, some of the sticky stuff adhered to the wings, Dr. Ruschi would remove it with an application of lighter fluid, grasping the bird by the beak so that the mad flutter of its wings would evaporate the excess fluid.

As the final act, Dr. Ruschi produces a small strip of muslin with a slit in the middle, pops the bird's head through the slit and carefully wraps the muslin over the wings to prevent their beating, finally tying the package up neatly with a bit of string. After giving the bird a nip from a feeding bottle he stores it away nonchalantly in his shirt pocket.

One would never have believed that the birds would tolerate such handling—but I have seen him go through his routine dozens of times and no harm ever came to the birds. When finally released into his large aviary, they buzzed away as if nothing had happened.

Our own first (and last) experience with hummingbirds in nightshirts came when a friend of Dr. Ruschi's in Rio asked us if we would take him some birds when we went to visit him in Santa Teresa. We said we'd be glad to, of course. The friend met us at the airport the next morning with a shoe box containing ten hummingbirds in their night-shirts, arranged in neat rows together with a feeder containing ample food for the journey. Our instructions were to feed once every half hour. The performance created quite a stir in the airplane. The feeding process (with the shoe box on my lap) attracted first the stewardess, then the passengers, and finally the pilot and co-pilot (fortunately on separate occasions). All were enchanted with our small charges and told us all about it in torrents of excited and quite incomprehensible Portuguese. Quite a few hours later we turned our precious package over to Dr. Ruschi in Santa Teresa—with a sigh of relief. He released the prisoners into the large aviary, and off they flew, apparently without a care.

To return now to photography, the principal problem is to make the birds approach the camera in a way that shows them off to best advantage. If a picture from the side will serve, the difficulty is not great. The spout of the feeder is turned so that the birds approach it across the field of view of the camera, the beam of light is centered in the picture area and one simply waits and presses buttons.

The head-on shots required to show the iridescent gorget, call for more ingenuity, however. Here one places the spout of the feeder at the center of the lower edge of the picture area and tilts the feeder and camera so that the picture is taken at an angle 15 or 20 degrees below the horizontal. The photocell is placed on the center line of the picture area (out of sight, of course) and just far enough back of the spout of the feeder so that the beam will not be interrupted when the bird is feeding, but will be triggered by the bird's tail when it rises and backs away from the feeder. This is a chancy business and the percentages are far from favorable to the photographer.

When the feature is a long iridescent tail or back, one must use a perch and somehow persuade the bird to turn his back. This is done by adjusting the spout of the feeder to such a position that the bird may feed in greatest comfort with his back to the camera. Also, by placing the beam of light close to the perch, one can frequently get pictures of the arrival or take-off.

However much one contrives, getting a really good picture is simply a matter of statistics. The flash is far faster than the eye and one never knows before actually seeing the transparency whether the picture is good or not. I simply take pictures continuously quite regardless of the film consumed and hope that when I get home and see the final results, I will find that Fortune has smiled and I have three or four really good shots. Sometimes she smiles and sometimes she doesn't. It took four tries on four separate excursions to get a really good picture of the male *Chrysolampis mosquitus,* and as for *Biossonneaua jardini,* I still lack a picture that shows his iridescent parts in all their glory. For *Cynanthus latirostris* the story was quite different. I took 15 pictures in all and each of them was excellent. So it goes!

The ideal head-on picture, for example, is one in which the gorget shines, the wings are nicely spread, the tail is open to show shape and coloring and the head is turned to a three-quarter view (if the beak is directly head-on it is foreshortened to the point of invisibility). And every part, of course, must be perfectly in focus.

I would guess that overall the odds in the photographer's favor are no better than one in thirty. For those who are statistically minded, the color plates presented here were selected from about fifteen thousand transparencies. For some species there was only one usable choice, for others there were dozens, one about as good as another.

So there we are. In retrospect, it all seems very simple—but there were many headaches on the way, and problems which at first seemed insuperable. I would say that the first and most important ingredient for the successful photography of these delightful birds is patience and the willingness to fail and try again. The second requirement is an abundance of friends willing to be helpful whether the problem is bird finding or apparatus building. Here I have been particularly blessed.

I write finis to the project with mixed feelings. In one way I'm glad it's over, with at least something to show for several years of effort. In another way I wish I were starting all over again and packing up for my first expedition.

The mixed feelings here balance out, I suppose. But of one thing I'm sure—whatever the alternative, I wouldn't have missed a minute.

ACKNOWLEDGMENTS

General Ornithological

Dr. Dean Amadon, Lamont Curator of Birds, The American Museum of Natural History, whose encouragement and assistance since the inception of the project did much to insure ultimate success.

Mr. E. Thomas Gilliard, who accompanied us on our first expedition to Venezuela and whose assistance was invaluable there, and at many other times.

Dr. Wesley E. Lanyon, Dr. Charles Vaurie, and Mr. Charles E. O'Brien, all of whom provided data and information both promptly and cheerfully.

Captain Jean Delacour, whose suggestion led me to Dr. Beraut and Dr. Ruschi, both "treasure troves" of hummingbird lore.

Dr. William C. Dilger, whose creative advice improved the quality of the black-and-white drawings in Chapter 1.

Electronic Flash Equipment

Professor Harold E. Edgerton, "Papa Flash" himself, whose contributions, too numerous to list, helped to produce a compact, extremely high-speed electronic flash unit.

General Electronics

Mr. Victor F. Hanson, whose contributions I have mentioned in the Preface, and who, as an extra, provided in his garden a male ruby throat whose photograph appears herein as Plate 1.

Mr. Hanson's associates, Messrs. Paul C. Hoell, Jean M. Morris, and Ronald P. Schwenker, who would produce on call and with great dispatch any conceivable piece of electronic gear, no matter how complex.

Iridescence

Mr. Daniel D. Friel, who designed and constructed the equipment used in the study of iridescent colors and whose advice and assistance as the study proceeded were of much importance.

Dr. A. F. Turner, a leading expert on interference colors, who contributed greatly to our theoretical understanding of these phenomena.

Dr. Werner Brandt, who with his very great mathematical abilities provided the theoretical analysis of inhomogeneous interference and who, as an entirely unexpected bonus, contributed much to the development of oscillator theory in its application to flying animals.

High-Speed Motion Picture Camera

Mr. W. O. Johnson and Mr. Robert Kerr, who designed the high-speed motion picture camera described in Chapter 3.

Wind Tunnel

Mr. Harcourt C. Vernon, who designed and constructed "Daddy's torture chamber".

Aerodynamics

Professor R. H. Miller and his associate, Professor Erik Mollø-Christiansen, who were kind enough to lead me through the wilderness of aerodynamics as applied to the flight of birds.

In The Field

Arizona

Mr. and Mrs. James M. Gates, who planned our trip to Arizona and provided not only accommodations but a substantial number of well-attended feeders.

Mrs. Harriet Alexander, at whose cottage in Madera Canyon we photographed *Eugenes fulgens* of the purple crown.

Mr. and Mrs. Thomas St. John, who were kind enough to take me in for the night and at whose feeders I photographed all of the native Arizona species.

Brazil

Dr. and Mrs. Augusto Ruschi, whose many contributions I have endeavored to acknowledge in the Preface.

Dr. and Mrs. Etienne Béraut, whose gracious hospitality and friendly advice did much to make our three Brazilian expeditions so successful.

Mr. and Mrs. René Cassinelli, who gave us our first glimpse of the beauties of Brazil from their delightful summer home in Petropolis, where we photographed our first Brazilian hummingbirds.

Mr. Frank L. McClure, whose help in easing the Brazilian customs procedures and whose thoughtfulness in many other ways made our visits to Brazil both expeditious and agreeable.

Mr. Charles W. Rule, whose pleasant companionship and fluency in English and Portuguese were most helpful during our three visits to Santa Teresa.

California

Miss Fern Zimmerman, who made it possible for us to photograph at the Tucker Refuge in Modjeska Canyon and who located for us many other feeding stations.

Mr. and Mrs. Norman Fleming, who were kind enough to allow us to keep house in their cottage in Modjeska Canyon.

Mr. Don Bleitz, who was helpful in many ways and who provided us with the *Costa* hummingbird which we had despaired of adding to the folio.

Mr. and Mrs. Glen Kennedy, at whose pleasant house at Camp Angelus we photographed the elusive *Calliope* and who gave us the extraordinary experience of photographing hummingbirds in a snowstorm.

Mr. and Mrs. Frank E. Moore, who gave us shelter at Redlands and who equipped us to cope with the snow which was unexpectedly falling in the mountains.

Colorado

Mr. Walker Van Riper, whose helpfulness in providing any desired number of local hummingbirds and whose encouragement throughout this entire project as President of "The Society of Trochilodographers" made our visits to Denver both instructive and delightful.

Mr. W. R. Willis, at whose cottage near Colorado Springs we photographed the elusive *Rufous*.

Costa Rica

Dr. Oliver Griswold, who collected and was kind enough to send me the Costa Rican birds which were photographed in my absent son's bedroom.

Ecuador

Sr. and Sra. Caton Cardenas, Sr. and Sra. Leopoldo Arteta, and Mr. Andres Cardenas, whose gracious hospitality and kind helpfulness made our visits to Ecuador a joy not only because the hummingbirds

were abundant and willing, but because of the opportunity afforded us to see in an intimate and pleasant way a very beautiful part of the world.

Professor Charles H. Sibley, who with his wealth of field experience found occupied nests galore and particularly the one of *Lesbia victoria* in the portfolio.

Sr. Carlos Ruales M., who was able to persuade his Ecuadorian friends to maintain feeders against our arrival and who was helpful in many other ways.

Professor Gustavo Orcés V., who contributed much kindly advice from his great store of knowledge of Ecuadorian birds and, perhaps most importantly, unearthed the Ecuadorian collector with his blowpipe.

Jamaica

Sir William and Lady Wiseman, in whose lovely garden overlooking Montego Bay I photographed the *streamer tail* which appears on the jacket.

Mr. Charles H. Blake, Dr. C. Bernard Lewis and Dr. John Parry, who were most helpful in providing both birds and hospitality when we moved camp from Montego Bay to Kingston.

Panama

Dr. Carl B. Koford, who discovered the nest of *Amazilia tzacatl* on the banks of the Panama Canal.

Venezuela

Mr. and Mrs. William H. Phelps, Jr., who not only provided gracious hospitality on two trips to Venezuela for us but were so hospitable to the hummingbirds that we found literally hundreds at their feeders to greet us on arrival.

The Book Itself

Mr. Charles M. Hackett, whose many contributions in editing text, in threading the intricate mazes of book design and in planning layout were invaluable in bringing this book to its long awaited and, I hope, successful conclusion.

Mr. Earl Goekeler, whose expertness in the field of color printing insured the best possible reproductions for the color plates.

Mr. Domenico Mortellito, whose sure sense of layout and design were of great assistance in planning Chapters 2 and 3.

INDEX

A

Aglaeactis cupripennis, 38, pl. 26
Aglaiocercus kingi, 36, pls. 21, 22, 37
     kingi berlepschi, pl. 22
     kingi margarethae, pl. 22
     kingi mocoa, pl. 22
     kingi smaragdinus, pl. 22
Amazilia, number of sp. & ssp., pl. 47
Amazilia tobaci, pl. 17
     tzacatl, pl. 16
     versicolor, pl. 47
Anthracothorax nigricollis, pl. 45
appendages, 19, 28
Archilochus alexandri, pls. 6, 7, 9
     colubris, 4, 5, 7, 25, pls. 1, 2
Augastes scutatus, pls. 32, 62

B

bathing, 13
beard, 20, pl. 20
behavior, 20–26, pl. 9
belligerence, 21, pl. 9
bill, 18–19, pls. 14, 31, 46, 63, 64
Boissonneaua jardini, 11, 35, 36, 157, pl. 35

C

Calliphlox amethystina, 12–14, 16, 128, pl. 66
Calypte anna, 21, 107, pls. 8, 9
     costae, pl. 10
     helenae, 8, 16, 19, 124, pl. 65
Campylopterus falcatus, pls. 23, 24
     falcipennis, pl. 23
     largipennis, pl. 41
     lazulus, pl. 23
Chlorostilbon aureo-ventris, pls. 48, 49
     ricordii, 25
Chrysolampis, 3
Chrysolampis mosquitus, 3, 30, 32, 35, 36, 102, 157, pls. 42, 43
climate, 3, 4, 28
Clytolaema rubricauda, 109, pl. 57
Coeligena torquata, pl. 27
     wilsoni, pl. 30
Colibri coruscans, pl. 55
     serrirostris, pl. 55
color, iridescent, 7, 8, 17, 19, 22, 27–48, 103–112
color, pigmentary, 8, 40, 48
common names, 2, 3
courtship, 17, 19, 22, pl. 54
crest, 28, pls. 20, 52, 67
crown, 17, pls. 13, 15, 21, 57, 64
Cynanthus latirostris, 157, pl. 12

D

dimensional similarity, principles of, 121
Discosura longicauda, pl. 60
distribution, geographical, 1–7
dyes, 40

E

eggs, number of, 23
energy output, 9–11
energy requirement, 10–12
Ensifera ensifera, 18–19, pl. 31
Eriocnemis luciani, pl. 36
     vestita, 106

Eugenes fulgens, pl. 13
Eutoxeres aquila, 18–19, pl. 34

F

family, survey of, 2–4
feathers, iridescent, 27–48, 103–112
flight, 13–15, 113–148, pl. 47
food, 9–13, 15

G

Glaucis, 23
Glaucis hirsuta, pl. 50
gorget, iridescent, 17, 31, 37, 39, pls. 10, 13, 16, 21, 33, 38, 46, 60, 64. *See also* feathers, iridescent

H

Heliactin cornuta, pl. 65
Heliangelus viola, 36, 109
Heliomaster, 3
Heliomaster furcifer, pl. 64
Heliothryx aurita, pl. 61
hovering. *See* flight
Hylocharis, pl. 12
Hylocharis chrysura, pl. 63
     sapphirina, pl. 46

I

incubation, 23, 24
iridescence. *See* color, iridescent

L

Lampornis clemenciae, pl. 11
Lesbia victoriae, pl. 29
Loddigesia mirabilis, 19
Lophornis magnifica, pls. 52, 54

M

mechanical-oscillator theory, 118–121
Melanotrochilus fuscus, pl. 58
metabolism, 9–13, pl. 8
Michrochera albo-coronata, pl. 15
migration, 6, 7, 13
molt, first, 26

N

neck, iridescence, pls. 60, 64
nest, 23–26, pls. 7, 16, 29, 44, 49
nestling period, 26
number of genera, species, forms, 4, 17

O

Ocreatus melananthus, pl. 39
     underwoodii, 6, pls. 39, 60
optical theory, 39–48
Oreotrochilus, pl. 20
Oreotrochilus chimborazo, 4, pl. 33
     jamesoni, pl. 33
     soderstromi, pl. 33
Ornismya falcata, pl. 23
oscillator theory. *See* mechanical-oscillator theory
Oxypogon guerinii, pl. 20

P

Patagona gigas, 8, 14, 16, 19, 124, 128, pl. 40
Phaeoptila, pl. 12
Phaethornis, 23
Phaethornis augusti, pl. 25
     hispidus, pls. 53, 54
     pretrei, 25, pl. 44
     ruber, 22, pl. 51
     yaruqui, pl. 28
photography, 149–158
pigmentary color. *See* color, pigmentary
plumage, 29, 31–39, pls. 4, 26, 45, 53. *See also* color, iridescent; color, pigmentary
Popelairia langsdorffi, 7, pl. 56
posture, day and night, 11

R

Ramphomicron microrhynchum, 18, 19, pl. 38
Rhamphodon, 23
ruby throat, 4, 5, 6, 7, 13, 14, 19, 22, 24, 29, 117, 130, 143, 144, 147, pls. 1, 2

S

Saepiopterus goeringi, pl. 23
Sapphirina, 3
Schistes geoffroyi, 17, pl. 32
Selasphorus platycercus, pl. 3
     rufus, 5, pl. 4
Sephanoides sephanoides, 7
size, 8, 16, 19
spectrophotometric curve, 105–108
speed, flight, 143–148
Stellula, 3
Stellula calliope, pl. 5
Stephanoxis lalandi, pl. 67
     lalandi loddiggesi, pl. 67
suspended animation, 10

T

tail, 6, 7, 19, 29, 145, pls. 21, 22, 37, 39, 45, 47, 52, 56, 61, 62, 65
Thalurania glaucopis, pl. 59
tongue, 12, 15, pl. 51
Topaza, 35
Topaza pella, pls. 18, 19
     pyra, 3
Trochili suborder, 1
Trochilidae, pl. 2
Trochilus castanurus, pl. 23
     ceciliae, pl. 23
     falcatus, pl. 23
     lazulus, pl. 23
     polytmus, 6, 101, pl. 14

V

vocal performance, 15, 17

W

weight, 14, 15, 19, 124, pls. 8, 65
wind-tunnel experiment, 129, 130, 143–147
wings, 13–15, 113–148, pls. 3, 23, 26, 45, 47, 49

Y

young, 24, 26